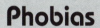

Phobias

AIM HIGHER WITH *PALGRAVE INSIGHTS IN PSYCHOLOGY*

Also available in this series:

Psychology of the Media

978-0-230-24986-8

Psychology of Addictive Behaviour

978-0-230-27222-4

Anomalistic Psychology

978-0-230-30150-4

Research Methods and Statistics

978-0-230-24988-2

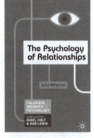

The Psychology of Relationships

978-0-230-24941-7

Biological Rhythms, Sleep and Hypnosis

978-0-230-25265-3

Issues, Debates and Approaches in Psychology

978-0-230-29537-7

Intelligence and Learning

978-0-230-24944-8

Sport Psychology

978-0-230-24987-5

Forensic Psychology

978-0-230-24942-4

Adolescence and Adulthood

978-0-230-29640-4

Health Psychology

978-0-230-24945-5

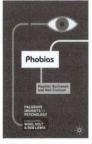

Phobias

978-0-230-29536-0

Gender

978-0-230-30273-0

To find out more visit **www.palgrave.com/insights**

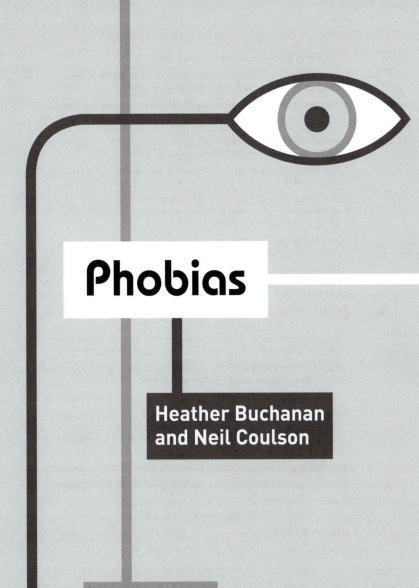

Phobias

Heather Buchanan
and Neil Coulson

PALGRAVE
INSIGHTS IN
PSYCHOLOGY

SERIES EDITORS:
NIGEL HOLT
& ROB LEWIS

palgrave
macmillan

First published 2012 by
PALGRAVE MACMILLAN

Palgrave Macmillan in the UK is an imprint of Macmillan Publishers Limited, registered in England, company number 785998, of Houndmills, Basingstoke, Hampshire RG21 6XS.

Palgrave Macmillan in the US is a division of St Martin's Press LLC, 175 Fifth Avenue, New York, NY 10010.

Palgrave Macmillan is the global academic imprint of the above companies and has companies and representatives throughout the world.

Palgrave® and Macmillan® are registered trademarks in the United States, the United Kingdom, Europe and other countries.

ISBN 978–0–230–29536–0

This book is printed on paper suitable for recycling and made from fully managed and sustained forest sources. Logging, pulping and manufacturing processes are expected to conform to the environmental regulations of the country of origin.

A catalogue record for this book is available from the British Library.

A catalog record for this book is available from the Library of Congress.

10   9   8   7   6   5   4   3   2   1
21 20 19 18 17 16 15 14 13 12

Printed in China

For Iona and Ailsa

Contents

Figures and Tables

Figures

Tables

Preface

" Fear makes the wolf bigger than he is."

German Proverb

We have seen first-hand through our research (which you will read about in the specific phobia chapters) that phobias can have a huge adverse impact on people's lives. As psychologists we continue to be fascinated as to how these phobias develop and the extent to which different treatments can be effective. In researching this book we also had the opportunity to encounter the enormous body of literature on phobias of which only a small proportion is covered in these pages. Indeed, this is not meant to be the definitive book on phobias but a student-friendly companion to take you through some of the main theories, research and issues. This book should introduce you to concepts that you may be unfamiliar with as well as further explore models and theories that you may have covered previously (such as the classical conditioning model), focusing on specific phobias, social phobias and agoraphobia. We hope that it develops a further understanding of this intriguing topic.

HEATHER BUCHANAN & NEIL COULSON
Nottingham, August 2011

Acknowledgements

The publisher and authors would like to thank:

Elsevier for kind permission to reproduce figure 3.1. Original source is Field, A.P. (2006) 'Is conditioning a useful framework for understanding the development and treatment of phobias?, *Clinical Psychology Review*, 26 (7): 857–875.

We are indebted to Amanda Robertson for her very candid reflections on her spider phobia (she is our case study throughout Chapters 2–4). We would also like to thank both the anonymous reviewer and Rob Lewis (Series Editor) for their helpful comments on the first draft of this book. Also, Nigel Holt (Series Editor) who made the first approach about writing this book (time for that beer now I think, Nigel). Thanks to Paul Stevens and Neha Sharma at Palgrave macmillan for helpful prodding along the way. Finally, we would like to thank The Peacock as a place of respite, reflection and refreshment during the writing of this book and HB would like to thank Kevin Paterson for being lovely.

Note from series editors

Being scared or wary of something is a very natural part of life, but a phobia is something else altogether. As you'll learn as you read this book, the range of phobias people experience is extremely wide and the impact they have on their lives is often devastating.

Heather and Neil make a formidable writing team and their collective CV makes for impressive reading. They came highly recommended and when they accepted our invitation to contribute to the series we were very pleased indeed. Both serious academics, with active international research profiles, Heather and Neil found time to construct a book that follows the guidelines we gave while going significantly beyond them. The result is compelling, interesting and highly readable, and also maintains an academic rigour and depth that is usually a great deal harder to penetrate.

- *You may be reading this book in preparation for university.* The study of phobias and the anxiety surrounding them is an integral part of courses on psychology. However, it is unusual to find the material so well focused and in one place as it is here. We are certain that this book will save you considerable time in your preparation while providing you with an insight that will give you quite a head start.
- *You may be reading this book while at university.* If this is the case, you are likely to be either an undergraduate or a post-graduate in psychology. You may be looking for that little bit extra to extend yourself a little, or for preparation of relevant coursework, or you may be looking for a friendly, accessible approach that will help explain material delivered elsewhere in your course. You'll certainly find answers here, which are in an engaging and extremely useful form.

- *You may be reading this as part of a pre-university course such as an A-level.* You will be more than aware of the competition for places at university now, and will be encouraged to go that little bit further and develop the knowledge presented in your textbooks. You'll also know the perils of including irrelevant material in your answers, and so we have provided directions to the most relevant material in the Reading Guide. This book will stretch and challenge your knowledge and really help you stand out from the crowd.

It may be, of course, that you are reading this book because you have an interest in phobias for another reason and this is absolutely fine. Textbooks can suffer from a lack of accessibility and dryness, but you'll see that this is not a problem here. The experience and knowledge Heather and Neil bring to this book is impressive and many academics of their standing have great trouble expressing their knowledge at different levels that can be useful to many readers. This is not a problem for Heather and Neil. We are extremely pleased to have this book as part of the *Insights* series and feel certain you will enjoy it.

Nigel Holt and Rob Lewis

Chapter 1

Phobia: An introduction

Introduction

Everyone at some point in life has felt anxious. Think back to the last time you felt anxious – the chances are you are able to recall an example fairly readily and that it is related to a particular event or situation. For example, we can easily recall the last time we felt very anxious and why. It was when we both ended up catching a horrible virus at the same time as the publication deadline for this book approached ! Once we recovered from the virus, we realised how much time we had lost and we felt very panicky and overwhelmed. However, the feelings of anxiety passed as we worked through how we were going to deal with the situation and although we had moments of anxiety in the lead up to the deadline there were no long-lasting effects.

It's normal to worry and feel tense or scared when under pressure or facing a stressful situation. However, what happens when the anxiety stops being 'normal' and significantly impacts on an individual's life? In this chapter we will begin to consider the answer to this question. In doing so, we will introduce you to the spectrum of anxiety disorders, within which phobic disorders lie. We will introduce the classification and diagnostic systems that we will consider in more detail throughout the book when we explore specific phobia, social phobia and agoraphobia in some detail. We will present a broad overview of the importance of exploring and understanding phobic disorders, including the high prevalence of these disorders, and the impact on the individual and wider community.

Following this, we will outline how we will discuss the phobic disorders across the rest of the book (Chapters 2–6).

In this chapter, we will briefly:
- Discuss how phobia differs from 'normal' anxiety.
- Outline and discuss how anxiety disorders are classified and diagnosed.
- Consider, the direct and indirect impact of phobic disorders.
- Outline how the phobic disorders will be discussed in the remaining chapters of the book.

When is anxiety 'normal' and when is it 'not normal'?

As previously indicated, anxiety is often an appropriate and 'normal' reaction to situations and events. For example, consider these three situations:

- You have to give a presentation or speech in front of an audience.
- You have a big party to attend and you walk in and can't see anyone you know.
- You are out walking in the country and you disturb a snake.

You may well experience feelings of anxiety in all of these situations; you would probably have had a rise in heart rate, sweaty palms and tensed muscles. This would be a typical reaction; it is normal to worry and feel tense or scared when under pressure or facing a stressful situation. Although these symptoms may be unpleasant, anxiety itself isn't always a bad thing – in fact, anxiety can help us stay alert and focused, and may ultimately help make that presentation or speech a good one. Anxiety is also the body's natural response to danger, an automatic alarm that goes off when we feel threatened. The *'fight or flight'* **response** is activated, meaning that your body is preparing itself to either fight to protect itself or flee a dangerous situation. For example, it would mobilise you to 'take on' the snake or escape from it quickly.

There is, however, a point when anxiety may become a problem and is no longer considered 'normal'. For example, consider these three situations:

- You are reading a magazine and there is a photograph of a snake.
- You have to eat a meal in a public place.
- You get on a crowded bus.

Most people would not feel anxiety when confronted with these scenarios; however, for some individuals being in these situations would provoke overwhelming anxiety. In these circumstances, a person is most likely to be suffering from a *phobia*. A *phobia* is defined as an irrational fear that produces a conscious avoidance of the feared subject, activity or situation. The affected person usually recognises that the reaction is excessive. For example, a snake-phobic would normally acknowledge that their anxiety reaction to a photograph of a snake in a magazine was not normal, and that the snake is not going to 'harm' them in any way. Nevertheless, this knowledge does not stop the 'phobic' reaction.

Phobias are classed as 'anxiety disorders'. In order to put phobias into context, let's consider how anxiety disorders are classified, and how phobias are placed in this spectrum of disorders.

◉ Classification and diagnosis

The term *anxiety disorders* actually describes a large number of disorders where the primary feature is abnormal or inappropriate anxiety. Within this section, we consider how these different disorders are classified and some of the debates surrounding the classifications and diagnostic criteria.

Anxiety disorders in the Diagnostic and Statistical Manual of Mental Disorders (DSM): A brief history

Anxiety disorders were recognised only in 1980 by the American Psychiatric Association (APA) with the publication of the *third edition of the Diagnostic and Statistical Manual of Mental Disorders (DSM-III)*. (See Box 1.1 for an overview of DSM). Prior to 1980, people experiencing one of these disorders usually received a broad or vague diagnosis such as 'stress' or 'suffering from nerves'.

The revisions of DSM that took place after 1980 brought major changes in the classification of anxiety disorders (see Antony et al., 2009, for an interesting historical overview). For example, in 1994 there was a major revision in DSM which coincided with the publication of the International Classification of Disease (ICD-10; World Health Organisation, 1992; see Box 1.1), and efforts were made to ensure some consistency between the two publications. In addition, there was even greater emphasis on grounding the changes in scientific research findings, rather than on professional consensus alone. A number of papers were published, outlining the empirical advances in anxiety disorders and championing changes based on these changes.

Box 1.1: Classification systems for anxiety disorders

In order to standardise the description and interpretation of mental disorders, diagnosis and classification systems have been set up. At present there are two established classification systems for mental disorders: The classification system of the American Psychiatric Association (APA), the Diagnostic and Statistical Manual of Mental Disorders (DSM), and The International Classification of Diseases (ICD-10) published by the World Health Organisation (WHO).

DSM covers all mental health disorders for both children and adults. It is periodically updated, and is currently on the fourth edition; an updated version was published in 2000 with some minor text revisions (DSM-IV TR). The manual is often referred to as the 'bible' for professionals who are making a mental health diagnosis. DSM is due for an update (to be published in 2013), and changes to these diagnostic criteria are being debated and compiled. Recently, feedback and comments have been invited from a range of people, including patient organisations and charities, therapists and research establishments.

The main focus of DSM is on the description of symptoms as well as information concerning which gender is most affected by the illness, the typical age of onset, the effects of treatment and common treatment approaches. The DSM-IV TR is based on five different dimensions (called axes):

Axis I – all psychiatric diagnostic categories, except personality disorders and mental retardation,
Axis II – personality disorders and mental retardation,
Axis III – medical conditions that are relevant to the psychiatric disorder,
Axis IV – psychosocial and environmental problems,
Axis V – global assessment function (GAF) that is assigned to an individual is a number in the range 1–100 and it determines the level of functioning and alludes to the need for treatment, level of treatment, as well as prognosis

This multidimensional approach allows clinicians and psychiatrists to make a more comprehensive evaluation of a client's level of functioning, because mental illnesses often impact on many different life areas.

The International Classification of Diseases (ICD-10) is an international standard diagnostic classification for all general **epidemiological** and many health management purposes, produced by The World Health Organisation (WHO). Chapter V in ICD-10 covers Mental and Behavioural disorder, including anxiety disorders. It is commonly assumed that diagnoses according to DSM-IV and ICD-10 are equivalent as both classifications systems converged strongly in their last revisions. However, this is not always the case. Although we will refer to ICD-10 within this book, we will mostly feature classification and diagnostic criteria from DSM.

Current classification in DSM: Twelve types of anxiety disorders

According to the latest edition of the Diagnostic and Statistical Manual of Mental Disorders (DSM–IV–TR; 2000) the following disorders are considered anxiety disorders:

- Panic disorder without agoraphobia – A person with this disorder suffers from recurrent panic attacks and worries about experiencing more attacks, but agoraphobia is not present. Panic attacks are sudden attacks of intense fear or apprehension during which the sufferer may experience shortness of breath, increased heart rate, choking, and/or a fear of losing control. Agoraphobia is anxiety about places or situations from which escape might be difficult, or in which help might not be available.
- Panic disorder with agoraphobia – A person with this disorder also experiences recurrent panic attacks, but also has agoraphobia. The anxiety about certain places or situations may lead to avoidance of those places or situations.
- Agoraphobia without history of panic disorder – The person with this disorder suffers from agoraphobia and experiences panic-like symptoms but does not experience recurring panic attacks.
- Specific phobias – A person diagnosed with a specific phobia suffers from extreme anxiety when he or she is exposed to a particular object or situation. The feared stimuli may include particular

animals (dogs, spiders, snakes, etc.), situations (crossing bridges, driving through tunnels), storms, heights and many others.

- Social phobia – A person with social phobia fears social situations or situations in which the individual is expected to perform. These situations may include eating in public or speaking in public, for example.

- Obsessive-compulsive disorder – A person with this disorder feels anxiety in the presence of a certain stimulus or situation, and feels compelled to perform an act (a compulsion) to neutralise the anxiety. For example, upon touching a doorknob, a person may feel compelled to wash his or her hands four times, or more.

- Post-traumatic stress disorder – This disorder may be diagnosed after a person has experienced a traumatic event, and long after the event, the person still mentally re-experiences the event along with the same feelings of anxiety that the original event produced.

- Acute stress disorder – Disorder with symptoms similar to post-traumatic stress disorder, but is experienced immediately after the traumatic event. If this disorder persists longer than one month, the diagnosis may be changed to post-traumatic stress disorder.

- Generalised anxiety disorder – A person who has experienced six months or more of persistent and excessive worry and anxiety may receive this diagnosis.

- Anxiety due to a general medical condition – Anxiety that the clinician deems is caused by a medical condition.

- Substance-induced anxiety disorder – Symptoms of anxiety that are caused by a drug, a medication or a toxin.

- Anxiety disorder not otherwise specified – This diagnosis may be given when a patient's symptoms do not meet the exact criteria of each of the above disorder as specified by DSM-IV-TR.

Out of these anxiety disorders you will see that there are several that are related specifically to *phobia*. These are sometimes referred to as 'phobic disorders' and comprise social phobia (also called social anxiety disorder), specific phobia and agoraphobia.

◉ Diagnostic criteria for phobic disorders

As with all types of anxiety disorders, there are specific diagnostic criteria (provided by DSM) that have been developed to help determine whether

Specific phobia	Social phobia
The individual experiences excessive and persistent fear of *a specific object or situation*	A persistent and intense fear *of one or more social situations, due to a fear of showing anxiety symptoms or acting in an embarrassing way*
Exposure to the feared situation results in an intense anxiety reaction	Exposure to the feared situation results in an intense anxiety reaction
Adults recognise that their fear is out of proportion, although children may lack this insight	Adults recognise that their fear is out of proportion, although children may lack this insight.
The sufferer goes out of his or her way to avoid the situation. The situation can be endured only with great distress	The sufferer goes out of his or her way to avoid the situation. The situation can be endured only with great distress
The phobia severely impacts the sufferer's personal, work or school life	The phobia severely impacts the sufferer's personal, work or school life
In children and teens, the phobia has lasted at least six months	In children and teens, the phobia has lasted at least six months.
The person's fear, panic and avoidance are not better explained by another disorder	The person's fear, panic and avoidance are not better explained by another disorder.

Table 1.1 Diagnostic criteria for specific and social phobias

someone suffers from a phobic disorder. Although Chapters 2, 5 and 6 will cover these in some detail, we have presented a brief overview of the diagnostic criteria for two different phobias – social phobia and specific phobia (Table 1.1). As can be seen, there is a great deal of overlap between these phobias. Indeed, there is only one set of diagnostic criteria that differentiates between the two phobias – the target of their fear. However, as we will discuss further on in this chapter, it is potentially a very important difference in terms of impact on the everyday life of the sufferer as well as the effect the phobia might have on their friends and family and wider society.

It is important to have diagnostic criteria, as they can help in reaching a diagnosis and will inform how patients should be treated. However, it should be noted that there is ongoing debate surrounding these. DSM does reflect changes in subsequent revisions if there is strong evidence and a clear rationale (as evidenced by our earlier brief historical overview of DSM). Indeed, when we discuss the classification of specific phobia, social phobia and in particular agoraphobia in more detail in the later chapters, we will see that there have been changes throughout the revisions of DSM.

Section summary

Phobias (or phobic disorders) are classified under the larger umbrella of 'Anxiety Disorders'. There is specific classification and diagnostic criteria for each anxiety disorder in order to standardise the description and interpretation of mental disorders (provided by DSM) although there continues to be debate surrounding these.

Why should we be interested in phobic disorders?

So far, we have established that anxiety disorders can be classified into 12 disorders with specific diagnostic criteria. Within this, four are related to phobia. In this section, we consider the importance of exploring and understanding these disorders. As such, we will briefly consider the prevalence of phobic disorders and the impact they have on the individual and the wider community.

How common are phobic disorders?

Collectively, phobic disorders are the most common forms of psychological disorder, surpassing rates of mood disorders and substance abuse. Within the phobic disorders, specific phobia is the most common subtype.

Box 1.2: Are we the 'anxiety generation'?

Does the high prevalence of phobic disorders internationally reflect the escalating pressures and demands of life? This may well be one contributory factor. However, a more pragmatic reason may be that, until recently, anxiety disorders were not formally recognised (as discussed previously); so many people were not being properly diagnosed or were receiving generic diagnoses such as 'shyness' or 'nervousness'. What are your thoughts?

The impact of phobic disorders on the individual

Phobic disorders have the potential to be very disabling for the individual sufferer. Generally, specific phobias are considered to have less impact on a day-to-day basis than social phobia and agoraphobia as the latter two phobias involve feared situations which are part of 'everyday life'. However, the direct effect on the sufferer will vary depending on not only the type of phobic disorder, but also the type of specific phobia, and to some extent the individual and their circumstances. For example, consider the two cases of individual specific phobias and sets of circumstances in Table 1.2. The diabetic- injection-phobic may potentially be putting their life at risk every day by avoiding injections. However, the UK-based snake-phobic is likely to feel little impact of his fear on a day-to-day basis as they are unlikely to come into direct contact with one (especially as they will avoid situations in which they might do). However, it is likely that they may also have a phobic reaction to images of snakes which do regularly appear in magazines and films.

Examples of the same diagnosis of a phobic disorder, and a change in individual circumstances, across phobias are also shown in Table 1.2. For example, the agoraphobic who has to take the underground to work (or presumably take significantly longer/more expensive means of transport) may have a different impact from the individual who can easily walk to work.

In the following chapters we will consider the symptoms that sufferers of different phobic disorders may experience. However, despite their different forms, all phobic disorders share one major symptom: persistent and severe fear or worry in situations where most people wouldn't feel threatened.

Type of phobia	Individual's circumstances
Specific phobia	Type 1 (insulin-dependent) diabetic with a fear of injections
	Lives in the UK and has a snake phobia
Social phobia	Wants to become a TV presenter
	Wants to be a self-employed web designer
Agoraphobia	Lives in London and has to take the Underground to work
	Lives in London and can walk to work

Table 1.2 Examples of phobias and individual circumstances

Impact of phobia: A social phobia celebrity case study

In the last decade, there has been increased media coverage on the prevalence of phobic disorders. In particular, there have been a growing number of celebrities who have come forward to discuss their phobic disorder, often with the focus on helping others to feel less alone and to remove the stigma of such a disorder. The Hollywood actor Kim Basinger has talked openly about her agoraphobia and social anxiety. Indeed, when she received her best supporting actress Oscar in 1997, television footage shows that she could barely speak although she had practised her speech many times. The American footballer Ricky Williams revealed how social phobia (also known as social anxiety disorder) affected his life (see Box 1.3). This provides a poignant example of how a phobic disorder can impact on all aspects of a person's life. In addition, it demonstrates that phobic disorders affect individuals in all walks of life – even an individual who on the surface seems to 'have it all'.

Box 1.3: The famous face of social anxiety: The Ricky Williams Story

Ricky Williams is a trophy-winning American footballer who had it all – fame, money and talent. With a successful career, it is hard to believe that this football star who played for crowds of 100,000 dreaded the thought of going to the supermarket or meeting a fan on the street. But that was the hidden truth. He described how at 23 years old, he was a millionaire and 'had everything' but felt isolated from those around him, because he couldn't tell them how he was feeling, and he didn't understand what was wrong with him. Often portrayed by the media as aloof or even an odd-ball, he would keep his helmet on during press interviews and shy away from fans. He found it difficult to interact with his young daughter or leave his house to do everyday jobs.

Williams later learned that he was actually suffering from social anxiety disorder, also called social phobia. The diagnosis led to a treatment program of antidepressants and psychological therapy, and he has since made a dramatic improvement. By speaking of his disorder, he hoped that others would seek help. He contends that if even one person gets help as a result of his story, then it will be like 'scoring the game-winning touchdown'.

There is no doubt that celebrities speaking out about disorders such as social phobia helps to raise awareness (the Williams story made it to the front pages of the most high-profile American newspapers). However, some commentators have not seen this portrayal in such a positive light. Moynihan (2002) noted that Ricky Williams was being paid by the pharmaceutical company that produces the drug he had been prescribed for his disorder. Moynihan argues that 'celebrity selling' is just one more way in which pharmaceutical companies are indirectly shaping public perceptions about conditions and diseases in which they have an interest. He highlights that the *British Medical Journal* has previously reported that some in the pharmaceutical marketing industry have described awareness raising for social phobia as a 'classic example' where corporate-sponsored campaigns help establish a need for a new drug by reinforcing the actual existence of a disease and/or the value of treating it.

Point for discussion: Do you think that celebrities should speak out about their psychological disorders? Does it help remove the stigma of mental illness or is it simply just a marketing tool to sell a product?

Beyond the individual: The far-reaching and varied impact of phobic disorders

We have considered the impact that phobic disorders can have on the individual sufferer; but are there wider effects of these disorders? Although the high indirect costs of phobic disorders are not as obvious as those associated with other psychiatric diagnoses (e.g., the psychotic disorders), there is no denying that they have the potential to have a significant impact beyond the individual sufferer, though this is certainly most evident for social phobia and agoraphobia. For example, social phobia entails significant economic costs in the form of educational underachievement, increased financial dependency, decreased work productivity, social impairment and poorer quality of life (Lipsitz & Schneir, 2000).

Phobic disorders, by their very nature, can isolate those who suffer from them. However, they are also isolating for members of the sufferer's family. Again this is particularly true for individuals who suffer from agoraphobia and social phobia. For example, it can be difficult to effectively explain the last-minute cancellations of attendance at social events, meetings and other pre-arranged appointments. Moreover, relationships between parents and children, siblings, spouses and extended family members can become strained when an individual suffers from anxiety. Family members may withdraw from each other and children may not understand the issues and feel that they are the cause of the family tension.

Co-morbidity in phobic disorders

Phobic disorders commonly occur along with other mental or physical illnesses and this can further impact on the mental and physical functioning of the sufferer. **Co-morbidity** is somewhat different across the spectrum of phobic disorders, however. For example, individuals with social phobia and agoraphobia commonly have depression and a history of substance abuse (particularly alcohol dependence) though this is not often the case for specific phobias. However, most people with specific phobia have been found to experience multiple specific phobias during their lifetime (Wittchen et al., 2003).

A good illustration of co-morbidity, and the debilitating effect phobic disorders can have on daily life, comes from the US TV detective, Monk. Monk (actor Tony Shalhoub) suffers from a number of different specific phobias, and the anxiety disorder **obsessive-compulsive disorder (OCD)**. His extreme case of OCD cost him his job in the San Francisco police department (where he was a rising star) and for a time rendered him virtually unable to function. Although his conditions have improved with treatment and support from friends, his OCD and many phobias – including germs, heights and even milk – pose daily challenges for Monk and the people around him. An example from one of the episodes demonstrates the number of specific phobias he suffers from and his own hierarchy of fear.

> [due to an escaped snake, Monk is standing on a kitchen table]
> *Captain Stottlemeyer:* I thought you were afraid of heights.
> *Monk:* Snakes trump heights. It goes germs, needles, milk, death, snakes, mushrooms, heights, crowds, elevators.

Section summary

In this section, we have considered the extent to which we should be interested in phobic disorders. We have established that there are a number of key reasons why they are important to explore and understand. First, among psychological disorders, they are the most common and as such they affect a significant number of individuals. Second, they can have a negative impact on individuals who suffer from them in a myriad of different ways. However, this can be dependent on the type of phobic disorder (specific phobias are often less troubling on a day-to-day basis than the other phobic disorders) and also individual circumstances. Moreover, there are wider consequences and implications that go beyond the individual sufferer such as the effect on the family, and financial and social implications (more specifically for social phobia and agoraphobia).

👁 Overview of this book

The purpose of this chapter has been to introduce you to the spectrum of anxiety disorders within which phobic disorders lie, including the classification and diagnostic systems which we will refer to in the rest of this book. In addition, this chapter has introduced you to specific phobia, social phobia and agoraphobia and why we may want to explore them further. Over the remaining chapters we will consider each of these phobias in detail. For each phobia we will cover:

- Prevalence, diagnosis and classification
- Development of the phobia
- Treatment of the phobia

Section 1 focuses on specific phobias, which are the most **prevalent** of all the anxiety disorders (and phobias). Hence, we focus most of our attention on this type of disorder (three chapters). Specific phobias are distinguished from the other phobic disorders we will be covering, primarily by the very specific nature of the feared object or situation and also by the focus of the fear. More than 300 types of specific phobia have been reported, which can be classified into several categories: Animal/insect phobias, natural environment phobias (such as heights or storms), blood-injection-injury phobias, situational phobias and other types (including travelling in a car). In Chapter 2, we consider in some detail the classification and diagnostic criteria of specific phobia and the presenting symptoms of individuals who suffer from them.

In Chapter 3, we consider the important question – why, and how, do some people develop a specific phobia (and others not)? Within this, we discuss the evidence for theories and models proposed to account for phobia acquisition. These include conditioning models, biological explanations and the role of cognitive factors.

In Chapter 4, we consider treatment for specific phobias. Individuals with specific phobia are much less likely to seek treatment than individuals with social phobia or agoraphobia, although treatment interventions are generally found to be very effective. In Chapter 4 we explore why this is may be the case. We also note that specific phobia is different from the other phobic disorders in terms of treatments employed. For other phobias, evidence-based treatments include a range of strategies in various combinations, including pharmacotherapy, exposure to feared situations, **cognitive reconstructuring**, relaxation training and other approaches. However, in the case of specific phobias, there is general consensus that exposure-based treatments are the treatment of choice.

In order to give a real-life edge to the concepts that we will be covering in relation to specific phobia we have a real-life case study. Mandy is a woman with spider phobia who has agreed to talk to us about her experiences of living with her phobia. Her experiences (both past and present) will help illustrate how specific phobia can impact on daily life and the powerful symptoms that she experiences when in contact with her phobic stimulus (spiders). In addition, we will see how her perception of how she acquired her fear relates to current models of fear acquisition. In Chapter 4, Mandy demonstrates that she is typical of individuals with a specific phobia in that she has never sought treatment for her phobia, and explains why this is the case. She illustrates one of the dichotomies (and challenges) of treatment for specific phobia – it has a high success rate for patients who present for treatment, yet patients rarely do as it means confronting the target of their fear.

In *Section 2* we cover social phobia and agoraphobia. In Chapter 5, we consider social phobia (also known as social anxiety disorder) and examine its symptoms, prevalence and associated demographic characteristics. In particular, we will focus on how a diagnosis of social phobia might be made and look at some of the common diagnostic tools available. As will have already seen in Chapter 2, there may be a number of contributory factors to the development of specific phobia and anxiety and within this chapter we will discuss some common explanations for social phobia. We will explore in more detail the popular 'cognitive model of social phobia' and how a person's thinking may be 'faulty' and how this could then be addressed through psychological intervention.

In Chapter 6 we turn our attention to agoraphobia, but as we will see, this is by no means a straightforward disorder. Rather, changes in the way in which it has been classified in the DSM have had important implications on how we view this disorder, particularly in relation to panic disorder. Furthermore, these changes have made it difficult to determine exactly the prevalence of this disorder. Similarly, for this disorder, we will consider some of the common explanations that have appeared in the scientific literature, before turning our attention again to common treatment options.

In summary, for each phobic disorder covered there are common elements that exist across chapters (e.g., prevalence, classification, measurement, aetiology and treatment). There are also key issues and debates that run through the classifications of these disorders, for example, the historical changes throughout the revisions of DSM. We provide Boxes to illustrate points or to give further information on a concept or to provide some 'food for thought'. However, there is also variation across the chapters, which take into account the differences between the phobic disorders covered. For example, the final chapter focuses on the controversies and issues surrounding agoraphobia, panic disorder and panic attacks.

Further Reading and Key Search Terms are provided so you can carry on your exploration into phobic disorders beyond this book.

◉ Further reading

Bienvenu, O.J., Wuyek, L.A., & Stein, M.B. (2010) Anxiety disorders diagnosis: some history and controversies. *Current Topics in Behavioral Neurosciences*, 2, 3–19.

Key search terms

Anxiety disorders; prevalence, co-morbidity, diagnostic criteria, diagnostic and statistical manual of mental disorders

Chapter 2

Specific phobia: Diagnosis and classification

👁 Introduction

Almost everyone has an irrational fear or two. Indeed, mild fears are common in the general population. Some get anxious at the thought of needles. Others shriek at the sight of a rat and some get flustered when they have to get in a lift. For most individuals, these fears are not major and do not impact on their everyday life. But for some, they are so severe that they cause tremendous anxiety and interfere with normal day-to-day living. From the Greek *phobos* (meaning 'fear'), a phobia is an intense fear of something that, in reality, poses little or no actual danger. In Chapters 2–4 of the book we will focus on *specific phobias* and in this chapter we will be discussing their diagnosis, classification and symptoms.

In this chapter, we will:
- Outline and discuss how specific phobias are diagnosed and classified.
- Consider the characteristics and symptoms that individuals with specific phobias present with.
- Consider the prevalence of specific phobias.
- Discuss the different methods by which specific phobias are diagnosed and assessed.
- Discuss issues related to diagnosis and classification, for example, reliability and validity.

What is a specific phobia?

Specific phobia is an anxiety disorder classification that represents unreasonable or irrational fear related to a specific object or situation (The Diagnostic and Statistical Manual of Mental Disorders (hereafter DSM), 4th edition text revision; American Psychological Society, 2000; see Chapter 1 of this book for details of DSM). Originally called simple phobia, the name was changed to specific phobia with the publication of DSM-IV. Thus, in some older research articles or books, you may find that it is referred to as simple phobia (and sometimes authors use the terms interchangeably). More than 300 different specific phobias have been reported ranging from ones that are familiar (most people have heard of arachnophobia, the phobia of spiders) to others that are less familiar. Box 2.1 outlines how specific phobias can be named with some examples. When an individual suffers from a specific phobia, the object of their fear (such as spiders) is often referred to as the *phobic stimulus*.

Box 2.1: Names for phobias

Generally, new phobias are named by affixing the Greek stem *phobia* to another stem that is usually from Greek or Latin.
Examples of common (and less common) phobias are given below.

Acrophobia – Fear of heights
Brontophobia – Fear of thunder and lightning
Catoptrophobia – Fear of mirrors
Claustrophobia – Fear of enclosed spaces
Equinophobia – Fear of horses
Gamophobia – Fear of marriage
Myctophobia – Fear of darkness
Ophidiophobia – Fear of snakes
Peladophobia – Fear of bald people
Pogonophobia – Fear of beards
Tapinophobia – Fear of being contagious
Xanthophobia – Fear of the colour yellow or the word yellow

'Normal' fears vs. phobias

It is normal and even helpful to experience fear in dangerous situations. Fear is an adaptive human response. It serves a protective purpose, activating the automatic 'fight-or-flight' response (Cannon, 1927). With our bodies and minds alert and ready for action, we are able to respond quickly and protect ourselves. But with specific phobias the threat is greatly exaggerated or non-existent. For example, it is only natural to be afraid of a hissing python, but it is irrational to be terrified of a picture of a snake in a magazine, or in a film.

◉ Criteria for diagnosis and classification

Diagnostic criteria

The term 'phobia' is now commonly used in everyday conversation, but in many instances it refers to a mild fear or strong dislike, rather than an actual specific phobia. As with all anxiety disorders, there are specific diagnostic criteria that have been developed to help determine whether someone suffers from a specific phobia, although as we'll go on to consider, there has been some debate about how useful these actually are.

DSM-IV-TR defines seven diagnostic criteria for specific phobia:

- *Significant and enduring fear of phobic stimulus*: Patients with specific phobia display marked and enduring fear when they encounter a defined situation or object (the phobic stimulus).
- *Anxiety response to phobic stimulus*: Patients with specific phobia display anxiety as soon as they confront the phobic stimulus. When they confront the phobic stimulus, a defined situation or object, patients with specific phobia may experience a panic attack related to the specific situation. Children may cry, cling, freeze or display tantrums when they express their anxiety in the face of the phobic stimulus.
- *Recognition*: Although adolescents and adults realise that their fear is unreasonable and disproportionate to the situation, children may not recognise that their fear is excessive.
- *Avoidance:* Individuals with specific phobia avoid the phobic stimulus or endure it with deep distress and anxiety.
- *Impairment and distress*: Individuals with specific phobia display avoidance, distress and anxious anticipation when they encounter the phobic stimulus. Their avoidance reactions interfere with their daily functioning, or they express significant distress about having a phobia.

- *Duration*: To diagnose specific phobia in a patient who is under 18 years of age, the duration of the disorder needs to be at least six months.
- *Not accounted for by another disorder*: A diagnosis of specific phobia is assigned if the phobic avoidance, panic attack or anxiety related to the defined situation or object is not better accounted for by other disorders.

There has been some debate in the literature regarding aspects of these diagnostic criteria. Oosterink et al. (2009), for example, highlight that the central premise of a specific phobia is that the severity of the fear should significantly interfere with the person's normal daily functioning. However, they claim that the criteria set out by the DSM-IV provides no gold standard of fear severity or clear threshold when a fear of an object or situation is marked, persistent, excessive or significantly interfering. They contend that this makes it hard to differentiate a fear from a phobia in clinical situations, particularly because individuals with specific phobias change their daily lifestyle so that they can completely evade, or at least reduce, contact with the object or situation they fear. They argue that this may also adversely impact on the estimates of **prevalence** in **epidemiological studies** (we consider prevalence estimates later on in this chapter).

Classification: Types of specific phobia

As mentioned previously, people develop phobias across a variety of different objects and situations. DSM-IV-TR divides specific phobias into five types:

- *Animal* (fear cued by animals or insects)
- *Natural environment* (fear cued by an object in the natural environment, such as heights, storms, water or the dark),
- *Blood-Injection-Injury* (B-I-I) type (fear cued by seeing blood, injury or receiving an injection)
- *Situational* (fear cued by specific situations such as driving, tunnels, bridges, enclosed places or flying)
- *'Other'* type (Some phobias don't fall into one of the above four common categories, and these are classed as *'Other'* type. Examples include fear of choking, fear of clowns and fear of buttons).

Should phobias be categorised into 'types'?

The decision to categorise phobias into different 'types' arose from research which showed that different phobias had distinct features. For example, some phobias differ in their physiological response, age of onset and patterns of **co-morbidity** (Antony et al., 1997). Despite the differences between phobias, there have been arguments made against dividing up phobias into types based on the premise that it is neither meaningful nor useful (Antony et al., 1997). Some phobias, for example, do not neatly fall into a type; it could be argued that a fear of bridges could equally be classified as a situational type of phobia or of an environmental type. Antony & Barlow (2002) question whether classifying phobias into types adds anything more than simply naming the phobia.

LeBeau et al. (2010) conducted a review, one aim of which was to establish whether the evidence continues to support the current specific phobia types in light of the empirical evidence gathered since the publication of DSM-IV. Their findings generally supported the current specific phobia types. They argue that one of the advantages of retaining the types is to promote further research on each one, which may clarify further differences in origin, process, **co-morbidity** and treatment. However, they do raise the problem of inconsistency in use of the types in the research literature. They contend that some researchers disregard the types and study individuals with specific phobia as a **homogeneous** sub-group; some focus on only one or two of the types as if they are completely separate; some select an example of the type category (e.g., spider phobia for the animal type) and generalise it to the general type. They call for greater consistency from researchers.

LeBeau and colleagues (2010) also argue that sub-types are not a diagnostic feature, but rather the clinician is given the option of specifying the type to accompany the diagnosis of a specific phobia. They contend that subdividing specific phobias aids research development as well as treatment; especially in the case of B-I-I phobia type which is especially responsive to a treatment that is uniquely tailored to its physiological profile (see Box 2.2 for a description of B-I-I).

'Other' type of phobias

Although much focus has been given to the more common specific types of phobias, it should be noted that we can develop phobias of virtually anything (classed under 'Other' type). Sometimes the phobias that individuals develop may seem strange or in some cases amusing (such as fear of buttons or balloons). However, the intense fear that is associated with the stimulus is as severe as it would be for more common specific phobias. In addition, the unusual nature of the phobia may make it more embarrassing to admit to, or talk about, as those 'looking in' from the outside find it difficult to understand or believe. An example of how remarkable we find unusual phobias is demonstrated by a national UK newspaper recently publishing a full-page colour article documenting one student's fear of buttons (known as *koumpounophobia*) (Wheeler, 2008). The student documented how touching a button would be like 'touching a cockroach'. Her brother would tease her by opening her mum's button tin and she tried to hide her phobia from friends at school in case she was picked on. Her phobia was so severe that watching an episode of the children's programme 'Button Moon' would be like 'watching a horror film'. In Chapter 3 we will consider how some of these more unusual phobias develop, but for now it is important to note that the same characteristics/diagnostic criteria are evident in less common phobias (e.g., avoidance behaviour) with sometimes the added psychological burden of fear of their phobia being uncovered or not being believed.

How do specific phobias differ from other phobic disorders?

Specific phobia has a unique position among the phobic disorders in that individuals do not experience **pervasive anxiety** and they do not seek treatment as readily as individuals with other phobic disorders. Unlike individuals with other phobic disorders, the fear of individuals with specific phobias is limited to defined situations or objects. In general, the feared object (such as a spider) rather than anxiety symptoms themselves is the focus; however, especially for blood–injury–injection (B-I-I) phobias and some situational phobias, patients can report fear or sensitivity to anxiety symptoms or the consequence of these symptoms (see Box 2.2 for a description of B-I-I). For example, individuals with B-I-I phobia may report fear regarding the potential embarrassment or risk of injury that may accompany fainting, rather than just the sight of the needle or blood (the specific object of their fear).

It can be difficult to differentiate specific phobia from some other phobic disorders, as several disorders have comparable symptoms. They include panic disorder with agoraphobia and social phobia (see Chapters 5 and 6 for details). It can be hard to differentiate situational type specific phobia, from panic disorder with agoraphobia. Situational type specific phobia is regularly diagnosed when the person exhibits situational avoidance without unanticipated and persistent panic attacks. In contrast, panic disorder with agoraphobia is diagnosed if an individual experiences an initial onset of panic attacks that are not anticipated and subsequently experiences avoidance of several situations considered triggers of panic attacks. Although individuals with specific phobia, unlike individuals with panic disorder with agoraphobia, do not experience **pervasive anxiety**, they may experience anxious anticipation when they feel it is likely that they will come into contact with the target of their phobia. DSM-IV-TR outlines differentiating factors as the type and number of panic attacks, the number of avoided contexts, and the focus of the fear. Sometimes it is necessary to give an individual a double diagnosis, that is both specific phobia and panic disorder with agoraphobia.

Box 2.2: Blood-injury-injection (B-I-I) phobia: A distinctive specific phobia

Natural human uneasiness about blood, injury or needles sometimes becomes a specific phobia, which can lead to serious disability if vital medical procedures are refused. Blood-injury-injection (B-I-I) phobia usually starts in childhood (Marks, 1988). It also presents with a unique anxiety response. The response to blood or needles has been found to be unusual in that it consists of a **biphasic** reaction during which blood pressure and heart rate first rise (as in normal anxiety) and then rapidly drop, leading to fainting. Treatment for this phobia is also different from those of other specific phobias. Drawing upon the unique response, an applied muscle tension method was developed and this involves teaching patients to tense the muscles of the body in order to increase blood pressure and reduce the likelihood of fainting when phobic stimuli are encountered, which has been shown to be very effective (Choy et al., 2007; see Chapter 4 for further discussion).

Section summary

In summary, individuals with a specific phobia are unique amongst those with a phobic disorder in that their fear is targeted at a specific stimulus. There are specific diagnostic criteria that have been developed to help determine whether someone has a specific phobia (as outlined in DSM-IV); in addition, there are different 'types' of specific phobias. Although there is obviously a need for guidelines in relation to classification and diagnosis, there has been some debate surrounding the utility of some aspects of the current criteria.

👁 Prevalence

How common are specific phobias?

Specific phobias are the most common of all the anxiety disorders – you may know someone who suffers from a phobia or have one yourself (indeed one of the authors of this book suffers from one although she's not going to tell you which type!). **Epidemiological studies** that have attempted to determine the **lifetime prevalence** of specific phobia within the general population show that 10 per cent suffer from one (Alonso et al., 2004; Bijl et al., 1998; Kessler et al., 2005).

What are the most common types of specific phobia?

- *Animal phobia*
  - The lifetime prevalence rate of animal phobia is estimated at being in the range 3.3–7 per cent (Becker et al., 2007; Curtis et al., 1998; Depla et al., 2008; Stinson et al., 2007; Wittchen et al., 1999). It is found to be one of the most prevalent types of specific phobia among adults, adolescents and children.
- *Natural Environment phobia*
  - The overall prevalence rate for natural environment phobias is in the range 8.9–11.6 per cent.. Height phobia is the most prevalent of natural environment phobias, estimated at 3.1–5.3 per cent (Curtis et al., 1998; Depla et al., 2008; Oosterink et al., 2009; Stinson et al., 2007).
- *Situational phobia*
  - For situational phobia, the lifetime prevalence rate range is 5.2–8.4 per cent (Depla et al., 2008; Stinson et al., 2007). In terms of particular situational phobias, fear of enclosed places has the highest lifetime prevalence at 3.2–3.3 per cent.

Comparing prevalence across types of specific phobias: Some notes of caution

LeBeau et al. (2010) maintain that we should be cautious when comparing prevalence rates across specific phobia types. First, they argue that rates may differ for males and females (we will consider gender in more detail below). Second, they contend that the way phobia is measured (in particular impairment ratings employed in the diagnostic criteria for determining the prevalence rates) varies across studies. In some respects this is related to one of the points made by Oosterink and colleagues (2009) earlier – they argue that in DSM there is no gold standard of fear severity or clear threshold indicating when a fear of an object or situation is marked, persistent, excessive or significantly interfering. With these points in mind, LeBeau et al. (2010) state it is difficult to determine whether the observed differences in prevalence rates are sufficient to defend the categorisation of types of specific phobia.

Influencing factors

Age of onset

We know that generally fears and phobias tend to begin at a young age (Öst, 1987); however this can differ depending on the type of phobia. LeBeau et al. (2010) establish that differences exist in age of onset for situational phobia (early to mid-twenties), height phobia (late childhood or early adolescence), B-I-I phobia (middle childhood) and animal phobia (early childhood).

Gender

Research has consistently shown that women report fears more often than men (Craske, 2003; Oosterink et al., 2009) and that certain types of specific phobia are more common in women than in men. LeBeau et al. (2010) summarise the evidence; animal phobia, natural environment (height) phobia and situational phobia all show higher prevalence among women than men whereas the findings regarding B-I-I are mixed (some studies showing higher prevalence in women, others showing no gender difference). There are various explanations for why this should be the case. One is that gender differences in anxiety disorders are due to women being both biologically and socially driven to avoid threats more often than men (Craske, 2003; Curtis et al., 1998). The difference may also reflect exposure among women and men to different genetic and environmental risk factors for the development of phobias (Kendler et al., 2008). It has also been posited that the difference is due to reporting bias, that is men tend to under-report fear. Support for this explanation has come from studies such as Pierce & Kilpatrick (1992). The authors asked non-clinical participants to complete a fear survey in order to indicate the presence of fears. They then asked them to complete the fear survey again on a second occasion, but this time the researchers pretended that their fears would also be verified by physiological means. Results showed that the men reported higher fear on the second occasion, when they thought that their fears could actually be confirmed. There was no significant change in the women's fear levels. This would appear to support the assertion that men under-report fear compared to women. This was explored further by McLean & Hope (2010) who replicated this study with a more **ecologically valid** experimental task, and also investigated the importance of gender role (masculinity vs. femininity) as well as biological sex. Surprisingly, men did not under-report fear compared to women, and gender role differences did not underlie this finding. The authors suggest that men and women may differ in how vulnerable they are for anxiety disorders, in ways that have yet to be captured by researchers. Alternatively, they propose that we may need to define and assess the influence of gender socialisation better.

In summary, gender differences are well-established but the reasons under-lying them are still not completely understood. As McLean & Hope (2010) note, anxiety research continues to move forward at a robust pace but our understanding of the gender effects have trailed behind. Future research may consider clarifying the nature of gender roles, so they can be assessed in meaningful ways to enable the gender effects for anxiety vulnerability to be captured.

👁 Characteristics and symptoms

When someone has a specific phobia, they usually realise that their fear is unreasonable, yet they can't control their reaction to the phobic stimulus. Even thinking about the object or situation they fear may make them anxious. And when they're actually exposed to the stimulus, the fear is automatic and often overwhelming. This may lead to restricted lifestyles and may impact adversely on health, depending upon the phobia type. There are many different ways that this can be manifested. For example, a pregnant woman with B-I-I may put her own health (and that of her unborn child) at risk by not getting a vaccine for swine flu. We know that individuals with dental phobia are more likely to have poor dental health than non-phobics, and have been known to 'self-treat' (including pulling their own teeth out) rather than attend for dental treatment. Individuals with a fear of flying may not be able to take a promotion if the new position involves a lot of travelling, or a spider phobic may be unlikely to holiday in a country known for the number, and dangerousness, of the spiders.

Symptoms

The general symptoms of specific phobias include the following: Feelings of panic, dread, horror or terror; recognition that the fear goes beyond what is considered normal and is out of proportion to the actual threat of danger; reactions that are automatic and uncontrollable, and seem to take over the person's thoughts; rapid heartbeat, shortness of breath, trembling and an overwhelming desire to escape the situation. Extreme measures are often taken to avoid the feared object or situation. This is demonstrated below, in Mandy's description of her fear of spiders (Box 2.3).

Box 2.3: Mandy: A spider phobia case study

Mandy is a 40-year-old married mother-of-two with a high-powered Executive position in an International company. She has had a spider phobia for as long as she can remember. She gives a brief account of her phobia below.

"Even thinking about spiders makes me feel anxious and ill. If I do see one I scream, suffer palpitations and try and get away as quickly as possible. It can be embarrassing in social situations (unfortunately very common) where I jump and scream and swear as I think there is one on me but it's only actually a bit of fluff that looks like a spider. I look like a 'nutter' but I can't help it – it is an automatic reaction.

At home my husband will get rid of them. However, there have been occasions when he's been away and it has been hell when one has appeared. One time, I was on the phone to my best friend when one appeared and I was hysterical – she tried to counsel me to deal with it using the vacuum cleaner. Although I tried, I couldn't bear to get close enough even with the vacuum's extension. So I phoned my Dad who drove 40 mins to get it for his [at that time] 37 year-old daughter! I still couldn't sleep in the room myself that night and slept on the sofa!

Career-wise it is also limiting as one opportunity could be to open a branch [of my company] in Australia. An excellent relocation opportunity since it is English speaking. But there is no way that I could even consider moving there, my head wouldn't let me. It's like someone saying you've got the opportunity of a job in Spider World!

If I hear one more time that 'they won't do you any harm' I will scream – I know that, I'm not an idiot, just someone with an irrational fear".

Section summary

In summary, specific phobia is the most common of the phobic disorders (and of all of the anxiety disorders). Although it could be considered a **benign** disorder since anxiety is **circumscribed** and alleviated when the phobic situation is avoided, the fear is unreasonable, automatic and often overwhelming, and it is excessive to a degree that it can interfere with many aspects of everyday life. In the next section, we consider these factors in the context of one common specific phobia – dental phobia.

◉ Phobias in focus: Dental phobia

Despite advances in treatment techniques and local anaesthesia, one of the most common phobias is that of dentistry; studies indicate that the general population prevalence is in the range of 2.4–3.7 per cent (Oosterink et al., 2009; Stinson et al., 2007). Indeed, a large-scale study carried out in the Netherlands found dental phobia to be the most prevalent specific phobia in the Dutch population (Oosterink et al., 2009).

The daily impact of dental phobia

Research findings suggest that dental phobia often has a significant impact on patients' lives. Firstly, individuals avoid going to the dentist, which can have an adverse effect on oral health (Schuller et al., 2003). Indeed, a vicious cycle of fear and avoidance has been proposed whereby feeling anxious about attending the dentist can result in non-attendance at regular appointments, perpetuating the fear further and being reinforced by the avoidance of dental situations (Corah et al., 1982). In those instances where a patient is able to attend the dentist, treatment may take longer, and as oral health degenerates treatment can become more complex (Corah et al., 1982; Skaret et al., 2000). Dental phobia can have a wide ranging and profound impact on individuals' daily lives (Cohen et al., 2000). Patients report significant psychological and social consequences of their anxiety or phobia; shame and embarrassment are common experiences (Buchanan & Coulson, 2007; Moore et al., 2004) with research indicating that patients often report widespread negative social life effects (Berggren, 1993; Buchanan & Coulson, 2007; Locker, 2003) and a threat to self-respect and well-being (Abrahamsson et al., 2002a, b).

In an analysis of messages posted to an online dental phobia support group (Buchanan et al., 2010) the social, psychological and health implications of this phobia are conceptualised by one of the postings from a member:

> I never smile during picture times, I am 43 and to this day you won't find a picture of me smiling. Before all my teeth got bad my top two have been turned in all my life, and now that all my teeth went bad, I was ashamed to smile or laugh and be me I am a happy person but I have been hiding behind my mouth, and I am like others here my self-esteem is shattered
>
> (Buchanan et al., 2010: 366)

Participants in this study reported details of how the phobia impacted on their everyday lives, for example not wanting to be photographed; surviving on a soft-food diet (while craving foods such as steaks and apples); talking with hands over their mouths and being unable to pass a dental office on the way to work. They also felt stigmatised and embarrassed by the phobia itself, and described how they struggled to tell family or friends; in instances when the phobia was brought up with a confidante the reaction was generally not supportive as evidenced by the posting below.

> In general I don't tell people of my dental phobia. However I work with a woman who is like a mentor to me we talk about everything and I felt very close to her. I told her about my dental phobia last week and she said 'Duh. No one likes going to the dentist, but we just do it. How simple can it be?' I tried to explain the extent of my phobia, but her response was basically 'grow up' I felt incredibly pathetic after talking to her. She has shared some personal things with me, including her depression, but I try to be sympathetic and

would never make light of something that was serious to her. Has this happened to anyone else?

Buchanan et al. (2010: 367)

Dental phobia as a 'type' of specific phobia

In DSM-IV, dental phobia is considered an invasive medical procedure and therefore part of the B-I-I type. However, it has been argued that dental phobia should be listed as a distinct type of specific phobia (De Jongh et al., 1998). Thus, LeBeau and colleagues (2010), in their wider review of specific phobias, evaluated the case for dental phobia as a specific 'type'. They concluded that based on current research evidence, dental phobia shares more similarities than differences with B-I-I phobia (see Box 2.2 for a description of B-I-I), and as such it should not be listed as a distinct special phobia type. They do note, however, that it may be helpful for clinicians to reword the diagnostic criteria of the B-I-I type by parenthesising the phrase 'or other invasive medical procedure' so that instances of dental phobia or phobias of other medical procedures are properly included.

Dental phobia as a specific phobia

There has also been debate as to whether dental phobia should be considered as a phobia at all. Bracha et al. (2006) suggest that 'dental phobia', as commonly applied to the experience of dental fear and anxiety, is typically a misnomer. They argue that most dentally fearful individuals do not view their symptoms as unreasonable or irrational and, in that sense, resemble individuals with **post-traumatic stress disorder** (PTSD). Further, their review of the research suggests that B-I-I-type of symptoms probably account for a smaller percentage of cases, and that a larger subset of 'dental-care' anxiety (DA) cases stem from dental experiences that are, at a minimum, aversive and/or painful, and at times highly traumatising. They propose that this psychological condition should be termed as Post-traumatic Dental-care Anxiety (PTDA), and should be classified as part of the Post-traumatic Stress Disorder (PTSD) spectrum in the forthcoming DSM-V.

Point for discussion

If someone experiences painful and traumatic dental treatment and goes on to develop fear and anxiety in line with the diagnostic criteria outlined in

DSM-IV, should this be considered a phobia? Consider the arguments for and against this diagnosis.

Section Summary

In this section we have provided an example of a specific phobia which is common and has a clear impact on sufferers' daily lives – dental phobia. This specific phobia affects individuals psychologically, socially and physically. Dental phobia also illustrates some of the important debates surrounding specific phobia diagnosis and classification of phobia 'types'.

◉ Methods of diagnosing and assessing specific phobia

There are various ways in which specific phobias can be diagnosed and assessed. Lang (1968) famously suggested that anxiety is indicated in three relatively independent response systems: physiological responses; language behaviour (subjective report) and overt behaviours (avoidance). Therefore, methods to diagnose and assess specific phobias tend to reflect one or more of these. These include clinical interviews, self-report measures, behavioural observation and physiological evaluation. For each of these measures it is important to consider (1) how reliable and valid these types of methods are and (2) in what context a method is to be used in, and for what purpose. Measures can be employed for both routine clinical practice, and for research purposes. Therefore, depending on the reliability and validity of the method, and the purpose and setting, measures will have advantages and limitations. We consider some of these here.

Clinical interview

Clinical interviews are the most common method of diagnosing specific phobias in the clinical context. A clinical (or diagnostic) interview is simply an interaction between professional and patient, in which a series of questions are asked to determine whether the patient meets the criteria for a specific illness or disorder. These can be structured or have some flexibility (as in semi-structured interviews) and can include different elements including patient report, **behavioural observation** as well as the clinician's own judgement to make a diagnosis.

Grös & Antony (2006) state that interviewers should first assess the presence of fear or avoidance associated with specific objects or situations and then explore the level of distress or discomfort experienced when the patient is faced with them. They explain that interview questions should be directed at specific clinical features, including the origins and course of the fear, the symptoms experienced (e.g., fainting), types of fearful thoughts (e.g., fearful beliefs), how far the individual's fear or avoidance is concentrated on the symptoms or physical arousal.

Often, the diagnosis of specific phobia is made on the basis of an individual's responses to semi-structured interview schedules such as the Anxiety Disorders Interview Schedule for DSM-IV (ADIS-IV) and the Structured Clinical Interview for DSM-IV Axis I Disorders (SCID-IV). These assist in making standardised and accurate diagnoses that incorporate DSM-IV by a systematic probe for symptoms that might otherwise be overlooked.

In studies which have tried to assess reliability of structured clinical interviews, the participant is interviewed by one clinician, while others observe (either in person or by viewing or listening to a tape) and then make independent ratings. These 'joint interviews' generally demonstrate high reliability because the raters are hearing the same account. Indeed, a recent study using 'joint interviews' (Lobbestael et al., 2011) has found excellent inter-rater reliability for specific phobias using the Structured Clinical Interview. A more rigorous test of reliability (test/retest) involves the participant being interviewed on two separate occasions by two different interviewers. This method tends to lead to lower levels of reliability because the participant may, even when prompted by the same questions, give different accounts to the two interviewers (information variance), resulting in different ratings.

In summary, structured clinical interviews incorporate the benefits of structured interviewing and help make more accurate and reliable diagnoses. However, in view of the sample sizes needed in terms of research studies, respondent burden, time and logistical constraints involving resources required, clinical interviews are sometimes not feasible.

Self-report scales

Self-report scales include those that screen for various specific phobias and instruments that assess the severity of a specific phobia. The most popular measure of screening for various specific phobias is the Fear

Survey Schedule (FSS II; Geer 1965) in its various forms. Individuals are asked to rate a list of objects and situations (e.g., snakes, heights, spiders) in terms of how fearful they are of it (on a scale of 0–6 where 0 = no fear and 6 = terror). Although the FSS has been the most widely used measure, it is not without its limitations. One criticism that has been made is the number of items it includes that do not relate to specific phobias (e.g., items relating to arguing with parents; life after death), which could pose a threat to the scale's validity. More recent measures that have been developed may in time overtake the FSS in terms of providing more comprehensive information regarding the most common specific phobias. Oosterink and colleagues (2009) recently developed a self-report measure, to be used in their research study to estimate the prevalence of dental fear and dental phobia relative to other common subtypes of specific phobia. In their study, one section of the questionnaire consisted of questions pertaining to the presence or absence of 11 common fears (e.g., injections, snakes, heights and blood). When the participants responded positively to having one or more of these fears, they were invited to complete the next part of the questionnaire. This part consisted of the Phobia Checklist, which focused on the question of whether the present fears met the diagnostic criteria for specific phobia in terms of the DSM-IV-TR. When all criteria were met, a specific phobia subtype was presumed to be present. This measure may be a promising screening tool for specific phobias.

Box 2.4: A comparison of two 'fear of spiders' questionnaires: Reliability & validity

Muris & Merckelbach (1996) compared two self-report measures of spider fear in terms of reliability and validity: the Fear of Spiders Questionnaire (FSQ) and Spider Phobia Questionnaire (SPQ). In the first study, participants completed the questionnaires on two occasions, 3 weeks apart in order to demonstrate test–retest reliability. Adequate test–retest reliability and internal consistency were found for both FSQ and SPQ. In the second study, the authors set out to test the validity of the measures, by carrying out a number of tests. The phobics carried out a Behavioural Approach Test (BAT) and during this they were asked to approach a live spider in a stepwise manner. There were eight steps, ranging from 1, 'walk towards the spider', to 8, 'let the spider walk on your hand'. After the pre-treatment assessment, phobics received one

2.5-hour session of exposure *in vivo*. Briefly, this treatment consists of hierarchically structured confrontation with spiders in combination with modelling by the therapist. After therapy, phobics completed the FSQ, SPQ, and went through the BAT again. Non-phobic 'control' participants completed the FSQ, SPQ, and underwent a BAT procedure. Both questionnaires were able to differentiate between phobic and non-phobic participants. Furthermore, FSQ and SPQ were sensitive to therapeutic change and correlated in a meaningful way with other subjective and behavioural indices of spider fear. Therefore, it can be concluded that both measures are reliable and valid.

In terms of assessing the severity of the specific phobia type, there are many measures available. Indeed, for some specific phobias, there are a number of different measures available; spider phobia, blood-injection-injury and dental phobia in particular have numerous questionnaires available. Indeed, Box 2.4 describes a study which compares two different fear-of-spider questionnaires in terms of reliability and validity (see Box 2.5). However, for other specific phobias (e.g., dogs, snakes, heights) there are a small number of measures available, but they are rather dated and there is little research available on them. Following our Phobias in Focus theme, see further on in this chapter for an overview of dental anxiety/phobia measures for both adults and children (Measurement in Focus).

Box 2.5: Questionnaire reliability and validity

In phobia research, selecting and using a questionnaire or measure that is reliable and valid is very important. *Reliability* refers to the consistency or repeatability of the measure. This is especially important if the measure is to be used on an on going basis to detect change (e.g., in terms of determining whether a treatment for a specific phobia has helped reduce anxiety). There are several forms of reliability, including:

- Test–retest reliability – whether repeating the test/questionnaire under the same conditions produces the same results; and
- Reliability within a scale (sometimes referred to as internal consistency) – that all the questions designed to measure a

particular trait are indeed measuring the same trait. For example, that all the questions are designed to assess the nature and severity of an individual's specific phobia.

Validity refers to whether the questionnaire measures what it intends to measure (e.g., the origins of specific phobia). While there are very detailed and technical ways of demonstrating validity that are beyond the level of this book, one example would be *convergent validity*. This refers to the degree to which a measure is correlated with other measures that it is theoretically predicted to correlate with. For example, a newly developed measure of specific phobia could be correlated with an existing phobia measure (only if the existing measure has been shown to be valid and reliable).

Psychophysiological assessment

Obvious changes in physiological systems, such as trembling hands, sweaty palms and pounding heart, indicate the importance of physiological assessments in specific phobias; yet in most clinical practice there is little actual use of physiological measurement (Grös & Antony, 2006). This is unfortunate because psychophysiological assessment can provide useful information over and above self-report and behavioural assessments. The under-utilisation of physiological measures may result from a variety of concerns regarding test attributes such as reliability, validity, utility and complexity (Orr & Roth, 2000).

There are various different psychophysiological assessments (e.g. peripheral measures reflecting sweat glands, muscle reactivity and **galvanic skin response**); however, heart rate is arguably the most commonly employed type of assessment. Measuring heart rate is relatively easy to do, and it can be recorded either continuously or at regular intervals across a specified period of time. Moreover, reliability and validity have been established over a number of studies. For example, two studies have shown that videotaped scenes showing spiders (Fredrikson et al., 1995) and snakes (Wik et al., 1993) elicited higher heart rate compared to neutral stimuli in individuals with specific phobia. Individuals fearful of driving showed higher heart rate while driving than non-phobic individuals (Alpers et al., 2005).

Although it has been argued that physiological evaluations are not normally used in routine clinical practice (Grös & Antony, 2006), the decreasing cost of equipment and training, together with growing research evidence supporting the usefulness of these techniques, has meant that it is now more feasible for clinicians to use these type of measures (Yartz & Hawk, 2001).

Behavioural assessment

The behavioural approach test (BAT) is the most commonly used behavioural assessment for specific phobias (Antony & Swinson, 2000). This involves observing or measuring a patient's responses when the individual is exposed to the object of their fear. The key is to do this in a controlled manner. For example, a snake phobic would be placed in a room with a snake on one side (usually in a tank!) and asked to go as near to the snake as possible. The clinician then assesses the fear response including behavioural response and fear intensity (on a scale of 0–100).

Grös & Antony (2006) report that this method can have advantages over the clinical interview, in that clinicians can observe the patient when they are reacting to a feared object or situation, which the patient would normally avoid. In addition, it is useful for clinicians as patients often over-report their phobic responses (Klieger, 1987). However, Cochrane et al. (2008) argue that there can be potential problems associated with BATs for both experimental studies and clinical work. They point out that researchers or clinicians are usually required to be present during the BAT to give instructions and to record anxiety levels; however, they may unwittingly influence the responses of the participants. This may even be the case when researchers are blind to the experimental condition the participant is in. Additionally, it could be argued that exposure to the phobic stimuli during the BAT may act as a part of the therapeutic intervention, making it difficult to tease out the processes of change from pre- to post-treatment. In order to overcome these potential threats to validity, some studies have used visual images such as pictures or video of the phobic stimuli as a screening device (e.g. Meng et al., 2004). Cochrane and colleagues (2008) have gone further than this, and have employed a BAT which aimed to provide a relatively precise measure of approach/avoidance without the participant actually seeing or coming into physical contact with the phobic stimulus (a spider). In their study, participants with varying levels of spider fear were asked to complete an automated eight-step perceived-threat behavioural approach test (PT-BAT). As in more traditional approach tests, a series of increasingly difficult tasks was constructed. The steps involved asking the non-clinical female participants if they were willing to put their hand into a number of opaque jars with an incrementally increasing risk of contact with a spider (unknown to the participants none of the jars actually contained a spider). The eight jars were laid side by side in a wooden frame, covered with material to obscure the contents. The lids of the jars were labelled as follows:

Jar 1 – Empty
Jar 2 – Had spider inside, now empty
Jar 3 – 20% chance of a spider
Jar 4 – 40% chance of a spider
Jar 5 – 60% chance of a spider
Jar 6 – 80% chance of a spider
Jar 7 – 100% chance of a spider
Jar 8 – Big spider

The PT-BAT appeared to provide a relatively robust measure of avoidance that discriminated between high, mid and low levels of spider fear on two behavioural measures: (a) the number of steps completed and (b) reported willingness to return and repeat the task. In addition, the fully automated procedure meant that the task could be undertaken without the researcher being present in the room, thus reducing any potential safety cues or social demands that may influence performance on the task. Therefore, good validity of this type of test is demonstrated. The authors point out that future research comparing this task with a traditional BAT may be useful in exploring the extent to which the PT-BAT represents a greater psychological challenge than actual threat in the context of fear and phobia.

Section summary

In this section we have considered the various ways in which specific phobias can be diagnosed and assessed, covering physiological responses, subjective or self-report measures, and observing behaviour. Within this, we have established that it is important to consider (1) the reliability and validity of the method and (2) the context and purpose. The next section considers self-report scales in the context of one specific phobia – dental phobia.

Measurement in Focus: Dental anxiety and phobia self-report scales

There are a number of self-report measures that have been developed to assess dental anxiety and phobia. Within this section we will consider some of the most popular measures for both adults and children. One important consideration when considering self-report measures for specific phobias is how reliable and valid the measure is (which we will also briefly consider here; see Box 2.5).

Adult self-report scales

There are a number of measures that have been developed to assess the nature and severity of dental anxiety and phobia. Although there are many studies exploring their use as outcome measures in relation to various behavioural interventions, their application in clinical practice in a survey of UK dental practitioners was surprisingly low, with only 20 per cent of dentists using adult dental anxiety assessment questionnaires (Dailey et al., 2001). However, since 2007, the Modified Dental Anxiety Scale (MDAS; Humphris et al., 1995) has been used as a screen for a number of dentists in Scotland, and there are plans to extend this coverage to the whole of Scotland. The MDAS comprises five items based on the dental experience (e.g., 'If you were about to have your tooth drilled, how would you feel?') and is rated on a five-point scale ranging from 'not anxious' to 'extremely anxious'; the cut-off score is 19 (indicating a strong likelihood of dental phobia; King & Humphris, 2010). Previous studies have demonstrated good **internal reliability** for this measure (e.g., Newton & Edwards, 2005) and it is used widely in research (e.g., Coulson & Buchanan, 2008). Other dental anxiety questionnaires are available, but tend to be of greater length and so are more suitable for research purposes (Newton & Buck, 2000).

Child self-report scales

It is important that dentists are able to assess dental anxiety in child patients as early as possible so that they can identify patients who are in special need with regard to their fear. It is also important that researchers assess dental anxiety in order to determine **prevalence** levels, correlates of dental anxiety and for determining the efficacy of treatment interventions. For these purposes, formal assessment measures are essential. Inevitably, assessing dental anxiety in children is more complex than assessing anxiety in adults. First, depending on the child's age, there can be limitations in what they can read and/or understand. For example, the term 'anxiety' is not easy to read or comprehend in younger age groups; thus employing adult dental anxiety measures are not appropriate. Also, children have shorter attention spans than adults; thus scales need to be brief and they should try and engage the child. Furthermore, the purpose of the scale should also be considered; if it is to be used by dental practitioners in routine clinical practice, it should also be simple to score and interpret. Therefore, assessment measures should be child-centred, quick and easy to use as well as reliable and valid (Freeman, 2005).

Possibly the most well-known measure is the Children's Dental Fear Survey Schedule (CDFSS; Cuthbert & Melamed, 1982), which asks children to rate their fear of 15 situations on a five-point scale. These are divided into (a) fear of invasive procedures, (b) fear of potential victimisation (e.g., from strangers, being afraid of hospitals in general), and (c) fear of non-invasive dental procedures. It has been shown to have good reliability and validity (Aartman et al., 1998), though its use in the dental clinic prior to treatment is not appropriate as it includes some irrelevant items such as 'having to go to hospital' (most patients are not treated in hospitals; Wong et al., 1998). Furthermore, the scale is 15 items long. Hence children may lose interest in completing it and this decreases the likelihood of valid responses.

To help engage children, and help them gauge their anxiety using a familiar response set, the use of faces has been incorporated into more recent anxiety measures. For example, the Facial Image Scale (FIS; Buchanan & Niven, 2002: 3) is a state measure of dental anxiety where children are asked to indicate how they feel on a row of five faces (see Figure 2.1; a higher score indicates higher anxiety) while in the dental context (e.g., in the dental waiting room, in the dental chair before treatment, etc.). It has been shown to have good convergent validity (when correlated with an existing child dental anxiety scale). The FIS also has a number of advantages; for example, it can be employed with very young children (it has been employed with children as young as three years; Buchanan & Niven, 2002). Moreover, the FIS is quick and easy to administer and provides immediate 'state' feedback to the clinician in the dental waiting room and could allow the clinicians to design appropriate

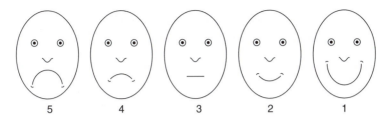

Figure 2.1 The Facial Image Scale
Source: Buchanan & Niven (2002).

treatment plans for their child patient. However, measures such as the FIS do have limitations; for example the amount and type of information which can be gleaned from this is minimal. It does not necessarily inform the dental practitioner, or the researcher, regarding *what* the child patient is afraid of. In order to address this, faces have been used in trait measures of dental anxiety (where children are asked questions how they would feel about a variety of dental-related contexts and procedures with faces as a response set) in both paper-and-pencil questionnaire format (Howard & Freeman, 2007) and in an interactive computerised dental anxiety scale (the Smiley Faces Program; Buchanan, 2005, 2010). Although these scales have demonstrated good reliability and validity and do have their advantages (e.g., the computerised nature of the Smiley Faces Program helps engage the child and facilitates scoring by saving responses to a database) they may not be suitable for use with very young children (unless helped by an adult).

◉ Chapter summary

In this chapter, we have established that specific phobias are the most common of all of the phobic disorders (and indeed all of the anxiety disorders). In addition, individuals who suffer from a specific phobia feel anxiety only when confronted with their phobic stimulus. We discussed the diagnostic criteria for specific phobia; most notably that phobic individuals will avoid the phobic stimulus, the phobia will interfere with their daily functioning and that they recognise that their fear is unreasonable and excessive. We have also considered how specific phobias are formally classified within DSM into five different 'types'. Although there is a need to have a clear diagnostic and classification system, it should be noted that there are debates regarding both diagnostic criteria and classification within DSM, for example, on the extent to which it is appropriate to specify different 'types' of specific phobia and on whether the diagnostic criteria are suited to some specific phobias (e.g., dental phobia). Finally, we considered the variety of ways we can assess the nature and severity of fear associated with a specific phobia. Depending on the purpose and setting (e.g., clinical setting; research study) behavioural approach tests, physiological measurements, self-report scales and questionnaires may be drawn upon. It is important to consider the reliability and validity of each type of method.

Now that we have established that specific phobias are common, that they affect daily functioning and that there is a variety of ways to measure them, we now turn our attention, in Chapter 3, to the following important question: Why do specific phobias develop in some individuals and not in others?

Further reading

Antony, M.M. & Barlow, D.H. (2002) Specific phobias. In D.H. Barlow (Ed.), *Anxiety and Its Disorders: The Nature and Treatment of Anxiety and Panic*, 2nd edition (pp. 380–417). New York, NY: Guilford Press.

LeBeau, R.T., Glenn, D., Liao, B., Wittchen, H.U., Beesdo-Baum, K., Ollendick, T., & Craske, M.G. (2010) Specific phobia: A review of DSM-IV specific phobia and preliminary recommendations for DSM-V, *Depression & Anxiety*, 27, 148–167.

Key search terms

behavioural approach test; phobic stimulus, diagnostic criteria, clinical interview.

Chapter 3

Development of specific phobia: Explanations and perspectives

👁 Introduction

In Chapter 2 we explored the characteristics, diagnostic criteria and different 'types' of specific phobia. We considered the different ways specific phobias can be measured and the high prevalence of this type of phobic disorder. In this chapter, we will explore the explanations put forward for how individuals come to develop specific phobias and how far the research evidence supports these explanations.

In this chapter, we will:
- Discuss the different psychological and biological approaches/explanations put forward for how specific phobias are acquired
- Consider the methodological limitations of some of the research on the aetiology of specific phobias

Psychological explanations

There are a variety of psychological explanations as to why some people develop specific phobias. In this first section we will consider the evidence for:

- Psychodynamic theory
- The classical conditioning model
- Vicarious/observational learning
- Information acquisition
- Cognitive models

Psychodynamic explanations

Like many areas of psychology some of these perspectives are best considered in their historical context. One of the earliest theories of why specific phobias develop comes from a psychodynamic or Freudian perspective. Psychodynamic theorists believe that phobias emerge because individuals have impulses that are unacceptable, and they repress these impulses. More specifically, Freud proposed that phobias emerge because of an unresolved **oedipal conflict**. The Oedipus Complex is where a young boy develops an intense sexual love for his mother and because of this he sees his father as a rival and wants to get rid of him. In terms of specific phobia, probably the most well-known Freudian case study is that of Little Hans who had a phobia of horses. Little Hans, Freud argued, was afraid of horses because the horse was a symbol for his father. For example, the black bits around the horse's face reminded Hans of his father's moustache and the blinkers reminded him of father's glasses. Freud believed that as Hans fantasised about being married to his mother he feared his father's retaliation. Therefore, Hans displaced his fear of his father onto horses because they reminded him of his father.

This is an interesting explanation for how the young boy came to acquire his horse phobia, but as with most of Freud's psychodynamic explanations it suffers from being difficult to disprove. The theory is difficult to test empirically and phobia researchers have tended to turn more to contemporary perspectives of phobia acquisition such as conditioning theories detailed below.

Classical conditioning

The behaviourist approach, pioneered by John Watson, was in direct opposition to the work of Freud. He believed that psychologists should adopt the scientific method, and study only things that could be directly observed such as behaviour and the environmental conditions that produce it. Watson's big innovation was to apply the idea of conditioning to human behaviour. This was a concept that had originally been studied by Ivan Pavlov in the late nineteenth century in his famous salivating-dog experiment. During his research on the physiology of digestion in dogs, Pavlov noticed that, rather than simply salivating in the presence of meat powder (an innate response to food that he called the unconditioned response or UCR), the dogs began to salivate in the presence of the lab technician who normally fed them. From this observation he predicted that, if a particular stimulus in the dog's surroundings was present when the dog was presented with meat powder, then this stimulus would become associated with food and cause salivation on its own (this learned response is referred to as the conditioned response; CR). In his initial experiment, Pavlov used a bell to call the dogs to their food and, after a few repetitions, the dogs started to salivate in response to the bell. The previously neutral stimulus (the bell) that now triggers the conditioned salivation is called the conditioned stimulus (CS), as opposed to the meat powder which is the unconditioned stimulus (UCS).

Box 3.1: Differences between the two kinds of stimuli and responses: The golden rule

It can initially appear a little confusing when trying to work out the difference between the two kinds of stimuli and responses. Try following this straightforward rule when trying to remember which is which; conditioned = learned; unconditioned = *un*learned. Simples!

Watson and his colleague Rayner (1920) initially showed how these principles could be used to instil a phobia into a young child, in the classic (though rather ethically dubious) study of Little Albert. Nine-month-old Albert exhibited no fear when initially presented with a white rat. Fear was, however, evoked when a metal bar was struck with a hammer behind his back (we weren't kidding when we said it was ethically dubious!). Two months after this initial test, Albert was presented with a white rat paired with a loud noise. After seven pairings Albert cried and avoided the rat whenever it was subsequently encountered. Therefore, Albert had learned to fear the previously neutral stimulus (the conditioned stimulus or CS, the rat) through its repeated pairing with an intrinsically aversive stimulus (the unconditioned stimulus or UCS, the loud noise). Over time, presentations of the CS alone (the rat) came to elicit responses like those initially elicited only by the UCS (the loud noise), that is crying and moving away. See Figure 3.1 for an illustration of how the fear is learned according to this model.

Classical conditioning has been one of the most popular explanations for the acquisition of phobias, and in many ways it makes intuitive sense. Fear results from the individual experiencing some initially neutral stimuli or innocuous event in conjunction with a traumatic event; the neutral stimuli then takes on anxiety-provoking properties. Support for the classical conditioning account of fear has come from a number of sources. First, the results of an array of experiments using animals have shown support for conditioning theory (Rachman, 1977, 1990). Second,

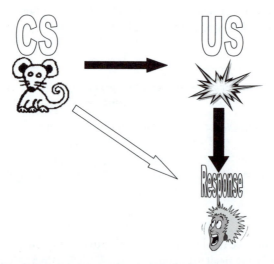

Figure 3.1 How Little Albert would have acquired his fear according to the classical conditioning model of fear acquisition used in Watson & Rayner's (1920) study
Source: Field (2006)

naturalistic studies support the notion that conditioning is a mechanism through which fears develop. For example, child survivors of a severe lightening strike (Dollinger et al., 1984) had more numerous and intense fear of thunderstorms, lightening and tornadoes compared to children who had not experienced severe lightening. Third, several studies have found that individuals with specific phobias consider classical conditioning experiences as being central to them acquiring their phobia (e.g., Di Nardo et al., 1988; Öst & Hugdahi, 1985).

Criticisms of the classical conditioning model in relation to specific phobia acquisition

Despite support for the conditioning model of the aetiology of phobias, substantial limitations of this approach have been outlined; let's consider the most common criticisms. First, many individuals with specific phobias cannot recall an aversive conditioning experience at the onset of their phobia (e.g., Withers & Deane, 1995). Even the research studies that do show support for recall of a traumatic event, normally have their basis in retrospective accounts and are therefore prone to memory biases (we will discuss further the limitations of retrospective accounts of already anxious adults later on in the chapter). Indeed, clinicians often have difficulty in finding out the aversive conditioning event that the patient has experienced, which is perhaps not very surprising considering this requires the identification of the US and its unconditioned response, and discovering when and where there was a matching of the US and the CS (Herbert, 1994). As the central premise of the conditioning model is the traumatic learning episode, this indicates a major limitation of this approach.

Second, only some individuals who experience a traumatic or painful event go on to develop a phobia. For example, World War II air raids produced remarkably few lasting phobias (Mineka & Zinbarg, 1996). Again, this is a criticism at the heart of the classical conditioning model.

Third, Eysenck (1979) noted that the classical conditioning model would predict that fear should decrease over successive non-reinforced presentations of the CS yet this is often not the case; in reality the opposite often happens. For example, an individual becomes phobic after being bitten badly by a dog (traumatic event). The dog phobic then has many occasions where he encounters dogs that are very well behaved, and do not approach him or behave aggressively. The classical conditioning model would predict that because there were a number of non-reinforced presentations of the CS (dogs) the individual would become less fearful of dogs. In fact, the individual often becomes *more* fearful of dogs not less.

Fourth, types of phobias are not equally distributed. According to traditional classical conditioning theory, all stimuli should be equally likely to enter into an association with an aversive consequence (the law of equipotentiality). However, we know from research findings that this is not the case. Phobias of spiders, snakes, dogs, heights, water, death, thunder and fire are much more prevalent than phobias of hammers, guns and knives; yet the latter group of stimuli seem to have a higher likelihood of being associated with pain and trauma (Seligman, 1971). As we will discuss further on in the chapter, some recent work has shown that fears are acquired more readily if the stimulus is 'fear-relevant'.

The classical conditioning model of specific phobia acquisition continued to be popular until around the 1970s, when these shortcomings began to be highlighted (Rachman, 1977). In response to these limitations, Rachman proposed that there are actually three pathways to fear; these are:

- Classical conditioning
- Vicarious acquisition through direct or indirect observations
- Information acquisition

In support of Rachman's theory, several studies have shown that a significant proportion of individuals attribute their specific phobia to either one of these pathways or a combination of these. Let's consider the latter two in more detail.

Vicarious conditioning: Can observational learning account for fear development?

Vicarious conditioning refers to the premise that individuals can acquire fear of an animal, object or situation vicariously, by witnessing another individual's fear of it (i.e., observational learning). For example, a child whose mother screams whenever she sees a spider may learn vicariously to be afraid of spiders. Indeed, Mandy the spider-phobic from Chapter 2 provides her thoughts on how she acquired her spider phobia, giving us food for thought in the context of vicarious conditioning (see Box 3.2). For all specific phobias, studies mostly report that vicarious conditioning is less common than direct conditioning but may be subjectively as intense as those acquired via direct conditioning (e.g., Merckelbach et al., 1989). For example, in Mandy's case, she indicates how her fear may be related to vicarious conditioning, yet the symptoms she describes (Box 2.3 in Chapter 2) are subjectively intense.

Box 3.2: Case study: Mandy's perceptions of how she acquired her spider phobia

There was no specific one event that I can remember for how my phobia started. I just remember that whenever my Mum saw one, she would scream, recoil and shout for Dad. And since spiders (I hate even saying the word!) are not uncommon, it was probably a constant reinforcement of the fear. Although everyone (annoyingly) tells you that they 'won't harm you', if your parent who is meant to be the big, strong, knowledgeable person in your life thinks that spiders are something to be afraid of, then as a child you think they must be frightening. This is why I'm trying so hard with my two young girls, as I know that my reaction will have an impression on them and I'd hate them to have this fear. And selfishly I hope they will be able to remove them for me when they are older – self preservation!!

Vicarious learning in animals

Some of the most famous, and indeed ingenious, studies on vicarious conditioning have come from the experimental animal studies conducted by Mineka and colleagues. In a series of studies, they showed that observational learning plays a powerful role in the acquisition of snake fear in laboratory-reared monkeys. These monkeys, who had never been exposed to snakes, did not initially show any fear of the snakes when they were first presented. However, they acquired a strong fear of snakes when they observed another monkey reacting with intense fear in the presence of a snake (e.g. Mineka et al., 1984). These studies provide compelling support for vicarious, or observational, learning in fear development.

Vicarious learning in humans: Early research in the laboratory

There is also evidence to suggest observation and vicarious experience can be influential in fear acquisition in humans. Early experimental work involved studies conducted in laboratories, where participants witnessed an aversive event (often an electric shock) happening to a **confederate**. For example, Berger's (1962) study involved participants witnessing confederate's reactions to electric shocks (moving their arm sharply) following a buzzer sound. Participants showed increased **galvanic skin responses** (GSRs) during observation and continued to show GSRs to the buzzer when it was later presented alone, demonstrating that participants had learned to associate the buzzer with the electric shocks and/or the model's negative response to the electric shocks. Although studies such as this demonstrate support for vicarious conditioning under controlled (laboratory) conditions, validity is questionable as the conditioned stimuli (e.g., buzzers) bear little resemblance to the conditioned stimuli common to phobias (e.g., spiders, needles). Moreover, the central premise in these laboratory studies is that the model (confederate) is physically hurt (by an electric shock). While this may happen in some real-world vicarious learning experiences (e.g., witnessing a school-friend being bitten by a dog) it is possibly more common that the observer is responding to a model reacting fearfully without that person being harmed (e.g., the friend showing fear in the presence of a dog, but not being bitten by it). A limitation to how these early studies can be applied to real-world phobias is also evident in respect to the durability of effects. As we discussed in Chapter 2, one of the diagnostic criteria for specific phobia is that the fear must have been present for 6 months or more. There is little evidence that the responses learned in the early experiments lasted for more than the length of the study itself (Mineka & Zinbarg, 1996).

Methodological problems in vicarious learning research

Askew & Field (2008) review the evidence for the vicarious learning pathway in acquiring phobias. Within this, they eloquently summarise some of the limitations of research, in particular, the literature that has relied on self-report retrospective accounts of fear acquisition. That is, asking individuals who already have a phobia to recall how they acquired their fear.

Firstly, Askew & Field (2008) highlight that many self-report studies do not include (either no fear or low fear) control groups, making it impossible to know whether particular types of learning events are more prevalent among individuals with fear and those without. Secondly, they highlight the problem of memory bias, which has also been a notable limitation of the self-report classical conditioning studies. They make the point that as specific phobias typically begin during childhood, with animal phobias having a mean age of onset of about 7 years (Öst, 1987), it is probably unsurprising that when asked as adults where their fear originated, many adults cannot recall a reason. We also know from research that memories are highly prone to changes or revisions based on experience (Loftus, 2004). Mineka & Öhman (2002) are fierce critics of retrospective recall, stating that investigators seriously underestimate the extent of problems that are generated by the unreliability of retrospective reports, generally 'only paying lip service to them in their papers' (p. 179). They describe one of the few studies that have attempted to estimate the magnitude of this problem. Taylor et al. (1999) asked driving phobics to indicate how they believed they acquired their fear. When they were asked to recall this again a year later, only 54 per cent of the pathways remained the same, with 46 per cent of the sample claiming a different pathway altogether! This demonstrates that retrospective accounts can be very unstable even over relatively short periods of time.

Box 3.3: The phobic origin questionnaire

A large proportion of the evidence from clinically anxious individuals has been obtained from using the Phobic Origin Questionnaire (POQ; Öst & Hugdahl, 1981). This questionnaire measures the extent to which the specific phobia was acquired relative to the three pathways; nine yes/no questions ask where the phobia came from in relation to direct conditioning, vicarious learning, informational events, mixed onset or no memory of where it came from. An open-ended question provides a forum for participants to provide any further relevant information.

Third, Askew & Field (2008) acknowledge that measures used to assess fear acquisition have also been subjected to criticism. They report that Menzies and colleagues (e.g., Menzies & Clarke, 1993a, 1994) have been the most renowned critics of the measures used, in particular the Phobia Origins Questionnaire (POQ) (described in Box 3.3). It is argued that the POQ overestimates the importance of direct and indirect pathways because of an inherent assumption that a phobia's onset is due to one of Rachman's pathways, which means participants are required to attribute the onset of their phobia to one of these or a mixture of these pathways (Menzies & Clarke, 1993a). In response to this, they developed the Origins Questionnaire (OQ; Menzies & Clarke, 1993a), which recognises non-associative accounts such as biological influences (which we will consider in more detail later on in the chapter) as influences in the acquisition of fear. The OQ has demonstrated good validity and reliability (Menzies & Clarke, 1993a, 1995), which has sometimes been a problem for the POQ (more specifically in terms of convergent validity; Menzies et al., 1998). For a brief overview of questionnaire reliability and validity, see Box 2.5 in Chapter 2. However, Askew & Field argue that there is an underlying problem for both measures – they measure an individual's beliefs about the cause of their fear, but this may not be the *actual* cause.

Vicarious learning and the development of fears in childhood

Field (2006) argues that it is generally well-accepted that fears can be acquired by observing others responding fearfully to a particular stimulus. However, he contends that there is little evidence that children can acquire fears this way. It is important to consider vicarious learning in children as we know that fears and phobias tend to begin at a young age (Öst, 1987) and that children have also had relatively less opportunities for prior learning than adults. The paucity of research may result from the ethical challenge of conducting experimental work with children, where the researchers are trying to instil fears in children. Earlier in this chapter we considered the early conditioning studies of Watson & Rayner (1920) where they induced a phobia of white rats in Little Albert. A study such as this would never get through an **ethics committee** today (quite rightly!). Nevertheless, in order for pathways of fear acquisition to be properly explored, there is a need for ethical experimental studies to be conducted, rather than using evidence from adult retrospective accounts only. Researchers, therefore, need to be inventive about the methodology they use in order to conduct this work.

Askew & Field (2007) demonstrate how this can be achieved. The authors conducted two experiments with 7–9-year-old children, where they explored whether the participants could vicariously acquire fear of three types of previously unknown Australian marsupials (the group of mammals commonly thought of as pouched mammals) - the quoll, quokka and cuscus. In the first experiment they explored whether vicarious learning could be demonstrated via children's self- reports of anxiety and whether the effects persisted over a three-month period. The children were randomly allocated to three **counterbalancing** orders. After assessing their fear beliefs, the children were presented (on a computer screen) with:

- One of the animals paired with a picture of a scared face
- One of the animals paired with a picture of a happy face
- One of the animals presented on its own

The animal paired with each type of face was different for each of the three **counterbalancing** conditions. Follow-up measures (including assessing fear beliefs again) were taken at 1 week, 1 month and 3 months later. Experiment 2 used the same procedure but this time it involved a behavioural avoidance task (BAT; please see Chapter 2 for further discussion of BATs) where there were boxes with photos of the animals on the front and soft toys and straw inside. Children could put their hand in the box, but not see the contents. Children were randomly assigned to a group where they were told either (1) the box contained the animal that had been paired with the scared face or (2) the box contained the animal that had not been paired with a face. Findings showed that children's self-reported fear beliefs increased for the animals they had seen paired with scared faces and that this fear persisted over time. Moreover, children were slower to approach an animal they had seen paired with the scared faces. Therefore, this study provides persuasive evidence that fear can be acquired vicariously, and as the authors point out this may be one of the first fully controlled laboratory studies in human children to show this.

Discussion point: Why might Field & Askew (2007) have chosen novel animals to test vicarious learning in fear acquisition in children in their ground-breaking experiments?

The role of information in phobia acquisition

The second indirect pathway to specific phobia acquisition (Rachman, 1977) is through verbal information. Until recently most evidence for the role of information in phobia has been based on retrospective recall of already anxious adults. As we discussed earlier, there are methodological problems with asking people to recall events that led them to become phobic, in terms of memory bias as well as methodological limitations of the questionnaires used for this purpose. A better approach is to look at the effect of information prospectively (Field & Lawson, 2003) and to investigate this in children (as Field (2006) similarly argued in the context of vicarious learning).

In order to do this Field and colleagues have conducted a number of experiments using child participants using a **prospective design** in order to test the effects of fear information in the development of fear beliefs in children. Their findings show that information can have a powerful effect. For example, Field et al. (2001) provided 7–9-year-olds with either positive or negative information about previously un-encountered toy monsters. Results showed that children's fear beliefs about the monster significantly increased when they'd received negative information about it.

Further studies improved even more on the Field's original **paradigm** by:

- Using real animals (unknown Australian marsupials; as described earlier in Askew & Field, 2007 above), and also employing a **within-participants** control condition to act as a baseline for a given child's tendency to change their fear beliefs
- Extending beyond the use of self-report only and measuring the effect of implicit attitudes to the animals to counteract **demand characteristics**. For example, Field & Lawson (2003) showed that fear information affects not only self-report measures of fear beliefs, but also behavioural avoidance of the animal about which information has been given and that fear information has an effect on implicit measures of attitudes towards the animals.

In summary, there is a growing body of evidence that children's fear beliefs and behaviour can be changed through information. Moreover, this work is methodologically rigorous, which has been a criticism of previous research conducted using retrospective recall in already anxious adults.

Cognitive explanations for specific phobia acquisition

A criticism that has been made of the explanations of fear acquisition described so far is that they do not take into account the meaning that people give to their experiences. There is, therefore, an alternative approach to the conceptualisation of fear acquisition. This approach, though far from unified, reflects a cognitive orientation.

According to the cognitive approach, people are active processors of information and think, plan and make decisions on the basis of remembered information. Cognitive psychologists contend that emotional reactions, such as anxiety, often occur in response to environmental stimuli or situations, but that these reactions are influenced by individuals' interpretations of the events, rather than by the characteristics of the event itself. From a cognitive perspective, fear is related not only to a biological preparation (see Biological Explanations further on in the chapter) or 'stimulus-response' association, but also to attributions regarding the safety and danger of the stimulus; the perception or control over the situation and attribution made about the bodily harm signal that stimulus elicits (Arntz et al., 1995). An essential role is attributed to an individual's 'cognitive appraisal': the interpretation of events and the perceived ability to deal with them (Lazarus & Folkman, 1984).

The past few decades have witnessed a wealth of work designed to advance our cognitive understanding of anxiety disorders and provide empirical support for theoretical claims, many of which were proposed in Beck and Emery's influential 1985 book, *Anxiety Disorders and Phobias: A Cognitive Perspective* (see Further Reading section at the end of this chapter). Although a number of cognitive theorists have proposed that **maladaptive cognitions** are significant factors in the acquisition and maintenance of specific phobias, it was Beck & Emery (1985) who encapsulated these into a comprehensive theory. They hypothesised that anxious people are mentally focused on threat as a result of the activation of cognitive **schemas** surrounding danger and harm. They contend that a sense of vulnerability lies at the centre of anxiety disorders, including specific phobias. When an individual encounters a potentially harmful stimulus a number of processes come into play. Similar to the transactional stress and coping model of Lazarus and Folkman (1984), Beck & Emery suggest that the individual makes a primary appraisal of the situation. If the situation is appraised as harmful, successive reappraisals are made concerning questions such as whether the situation represents an immediate threat and involves possible injury. When making the primary appraisal, the person is also appraising whether they have the resources to deal with the threat (secondary appraisal). Whether someone perceives they have the coping resources to deal with the threat is believed to determine the response of the person to the situation.

The major assumption of Beck & Emery's theory (1985) is that phobias result from a systematically biased interpretation of the future danger associated with a stimulus. An example of this is that fearful dental patients experience dental treatment as more painful than their non-anxious counterparts (Wardle, 1982). The common cognitive theme in beliefs and assumptions in anxiety is related to an overestimation of danger as well as an underestimation of one's coping abilities. It is assumed that once a **schema** is activated, it largely determines the individual's thinking and attentional activity. This would mean that when anxious individuals are confronted with their feared stimulus they would focus their attention to information which is consistent with their existing

schemata and ignore evidence that is inconsistent with their **schemata** and negative expectations.

Newer cognitive models of anxiety disorders share many central features that Beck and Emery had originally proposed, such as a **schema** or a cognitive set that predisposes individuals to process information in a biased manner, attentional biases toward threat, and catastrophic misinterpretations of ambiguous stimuli. Let us consider one of these models in more detail.

The cognitive vulnerability model

Armfield (2006) has recently proposed a model which is based on the notion of cognitive vulnerability and includes some of the key factors (e.g., controllability) that have already been discussed in relation to the cognitive explanation of fear. However, Armfield argues that researchers who take a cognitive perspective often lose focus of what is significant about the specific stimuli that lead to cognitive distortions. According to Armfield, we should be focusing on two key questions:

- Why are some stimuli more likely to be feared than others?
- Why do individuals with similar experiences differ in whether they acquire a fear or not?

Therefore, within his model he set out to account for the various characteristics of specific phobias and to explain both stimulus differences in fear propensity and individual differences in fear acquisition. The Cognitive Vulnerability Model (CVM) places emphasis on the cognitions of individuals, suggesting that the components of *disgustingness, dangerousness, unpredictability and uncontrollability* interact to create fear and are proposed to contribute to an overall vulnerability differentially inherent in people. Therefore, if an individual perceives an object or situation as disgusting, dangerous, unpredictable and uncontrollable, then a schema of vulnerability is created and a fear developed. While learning experiences may help shape these vulnerability-related perceptions they are not causal *per se*.

Does research support the cognitive vulnerability model in fear acquisition?

Research has shown that the CVM is effective in explaining spider fear. Armfield & Mattiske (1996) found strong associations between perceptions of uncontrollability, unpredictability, dangerousness and disgustingness and fear of spiders. However, Armfield (2007a) recognised that while it is often assumed that findings relating to spiders are generalisable to other animals and may be extended to other objects and situations entirely, there is no reason why this should be the case. Therefore, in a further study he recruited 162 first-year university students and asked them to rate their fear and perceptions of four animals that are usually associated with high-fear (snakes, rats, cockroaches and spiders) and four low-fear (rabbits, guinea pigs, cats and ducks) animals. The study had two significant findings. First, results showed that how the animal is perceived in terms of dangerousness, disgustingness, uncontrollability and unpredictability is related to subjective fear of a number of different types of animals (both 'low-fear' and 'high-fear' animals). Second, results highlighted that the strongest predictors of fear, and therefore the best predictors of the uneven fear distribution (i.e., some animals, such as snakes and spiders, are feared more than others) were perceptions of the unpredictability and uncontrollability of the animals. Importantly, familiarity with animals and conditioning experiences were not related to fear.

Although based on self-report, these are important findings; the schema (or set of thoughts) we create regarding different animals can explain individual differences in terms of who acquires fear. In addition, one of the enduring problems for conditioning theory is the inability to account for the uneven fear distribution in the population. Armfield's findings show that vulnerability cognitions strongly predict the uneven fear distribution of animals. He concludes that these findings demonstrate the benefit of investigating cognitive processes in relation to the fear experience and provides strong support for the CVM of the aetiology of fear.

Phobias in focus: Can the cognitive vulnerability model explain why some people become dentally phobic?

More recently, the CVM has been employed in a number of studies in order to explain the acquisition of dental fear. (For an overview of dental phobia, see the Phobias in Focus feature in Chapter 2). Previous researchers have explored factors that make up individual components of the model in relation to dental fear; for example, Milgrom et al. (1992) found that a lack of control was significantly associated with dental anxiety. Moreover, when Abrahamsson and colleagues (2002a) conducted in-depth interviews with a small sample of dentally phobic individuals, results indicated that the onset of dental fear was commonly perceived to be related to a threatened loss of independence and control, as well as to the unpredictable events surrounding pain. These factors are similar to the uncontrollability and unpredictability components proposed in the CVM, offering some support for these concepts in relation to dental fear acquisition.

Armfield and colleagues (Armfield et al., 2008) have recently conducted research investigating the relationship between cognitive vulnerability and dental anxiety with a large sample of the general Australian population. Their findings indicated that uncontrollability and dangerousness were independently associated with dental anxiety; however, unpredictability was not found to have an independent relationship with dental anxiety, which they proposed may be due to high **collinearity** with the other factors in the CVM. Whilst these findings provide some support for the CVM, limitations of this study should be taken into account. First, the authors used only a single question, 'Would you feel afraid or distressed when going to the dentist?' to determine the extent of participants' dental anxiety. Second, only the components of dangerousness, unpredictability and uncontrollability were explored to determine the relationship of dental anxiety with the CVM. Clearly, in order to test the model fully, studies should include all components. Third, only a single item was used to measure each of the three cognitive vulnerability components included in the study; a more comprehensive measure of the CVM components is needed to tap into these (potentially significant) cognitions.

Further research by Armfield (2007b) has more fully explored the concept of disgust, and found dental fear to be associated with disgust sensitivity (a specific difficulty regulating disgust); however there was no significant difference found between participants with low and high dental fear. Additionally, it should be noted that a general measure of disgust was employed (Disgust Sensitivity Scale; Haidt et al., 1994), which covers six different types of items/scenarios including food, animals, death and hygiene. Therefore, whilst general disgust sensitivity was explored, no measure was employed to gauge disgust specifically in relation to the dental context. In addition, Armfield (2006) proposes the CVM as an explanation of the *aetiology* of fear and phobias, yet he asked participants about their *existing* dental fear and whether they currently perceive the dental situation as uncontrollable, unpredictable or dangerous (Armfield et al., 2008). Therefore, whilst these findings highlight three of the four CVM components to be important within participants' current dental fear, given that the CVM is proposed to explain fear acquisition, there is some discrepancy between the findings and conclusions drawn.

In summary, the CVM is a relatively new and exciting model of fear acquisition, which has vulnerability cognitions at its centre. Research evidence has provided support for the CVM as a model of phobia acquisition, for example in relation to spider phobia. It also has some support as a model of dental fear acquisition, however research so far has suffered from some methodological limitations. Future research should test the whole model, using appropriate measures of dental anxiety/phobia, in order to comprehensively test it as a model of dental phobia acquisition.

Section summary

Within this section we have considered psychological explanations in relation to why some people develop a specific phobia including the three pathways proposed by Rachman: classical conditioning, vicarious/observational learning and information acquisition. We have also considered the extent to which cognitive factors are important. To some extent, there is evidence to support all of these explanations, although some studies have lacked methodological rigour. Next, we consider the extent to which biological factors are important in the development of specific phobias.

◉ Biological explanations

There have been a number of different biological explanations put forward to explain why some individuals develop a specific phobia. We will firstly consider whether there is a genetic basis for phobia acquisition and then go on to consider the extent to which there is an evolutionary basis for specific phobias.

The role of genetics: Could we inherit a specific phobia?

Could it be that we can 'inherit' a specific phobia from our parents? There is a certainly a large genetic heritable component in anxiety disorders in general (Boomsma et al., 2002; Hettema et al., 2004). Current genetic research is examining some genes that may be involved, first discovered in animal anxiety models and recently found to be applicable to anxiety in humans (Smoller et al., 2008). Some recent work has explored specific anxieties/phobias. For example, Ray et al. (2010) studied the genetic components of dental fear and anxiety in data collected for the Swedish Twin Study of Child and Adolescent Development (TCHAD) comparing dizygotic and monozygotic twins (see Box 3.4 for the differences between the twin types). They asked questions regarding their dental fear and intensity of the fear. They found that heritability of fear/anxiety was high in girls, but low in boys and that for both boys and girls dental fear intensity was highly correlated in monozygotic, but not dizygotic, twins. The authors conclude that there is genetic predisposition involved, allowing monozygotic twins to experience fear at a highly similar level, whereas dizygotic twins are not as alike, so do not share this. Although the authors acknowledge that a limitation of the study is that they lacked standardised dental anxiety questionnaires they suggest that future studies and theories of dental anxiety and fear must take the possibility of genetic vulnerability into account to a greater degree than has been the case in the past.

Box 3.4: Twins: What's in a name?

The difference between monozygotic and dizygotic twins comes down to whether they have the same DNA. Monozygotic twins, otherwise known as *identical twins*, originated from the same fertilised ovum, and therefore the same sperm. Only about a quarter of twins are identical. The more common dizygotic twins began as two eggs separately fertilised by two sperm, and therefore they do not share the exact same DNA.

Evolutionary explanations in acquiring specific phobias

The preparedness theory

From very early on, it has been muted that some fears may appear by **natural selection**. As far back as 1877, Charles Darwin observed his toddler son being frightened of large animals at the zoo. He wondered whether fears in children, independent of experience, may arise from hereditariness of real dangers during prehistoric times (Darwin, 1877). Seligman (1971) referred to this notion as 'preparedness' – that some associations are biologically 'prepared' or learned. According to this theory, we are predisposed to being afraid of animals such as snakes and spiders; we would then avoid them thus being less likely to become victims of their dangerous venom, providing an evolutionary advantage over those without this predisposed fear. This explains the fact that phobias are not equally distributed, as we have discussed previously (see Chapter 2) the most commonly feared stimuli are usually evolutionary threats (for example, snakes, heights etc.). A number of studies that have been carried out have supported Seligman's (1971) prediction that so-called 'fear-relevant' stimuli are better able to support certain features of conditioning (especially resistance to extinction) than are 'fear-irrelevant stimuli' (e.g. McNally, 1987; Öhman, 1986). Indeed, DSM now recognises that feared objects or situations tend to be aligned with threat at some point of human evolution. Also, if we return to the famous series of monkey experiments conducted by Mineka and colleagues, there is some evidence to support the notion of preparedness. Cook & Mineka (1989) found that when they exposed the monkeys in their experiment to monkeys who were displaying a fearful reaction to objects such as flowers or artificial rabbits this was not an effective means of inducing a fear; the monkeys in their experiment only acquired a fear of fear-relevant stimuli (toy snakes and crocodiles).

Box 3.5: Can spider fear be completely explained by biological 'preparedness' or are spiders 'special'?

Because all spiders are predators and most subdue their prey with poison, the preparedness theory posits that fear of spiders is an evolutionary adaptation. However, it isn't clear whether other **arthropods** similarly elicit fear or disgust. Gerdes et al. (2009) set out to investigate if all arthropods are rated similarly, if only potentially dangerous arthropods (spiders, bees/wasps) elicit comparable responses, or if spiders are rated in a unique way. They presented pictures of arthropods (15 spiders, 15 beetles, 15 bees/wasps and 15 butterflies/moths) to student participants who rated each picture for fear, disgust and how dangerous they thought the animal was. Results showed that compared to any other group, spiders were rated significantly greater in terms of fear and disgust, and spiders were also rated as more dangerous. Fear and disgust ratings of spider pictures significantly predicted the questionnaire scores for fear of spiders, whereas dangerousness ratings of spiders and ratings of other arthropods did not provide any predictive power. The authors conclude that spiders are special; spider fear is indeed spider specific. Their results demonstrate that potential harmfulness alone cannot explain why spiders are feared so frequently. They posit that the special reaction of spiders may possibly be explained by a combination of both cultural and biological factors.

Limitations of the preparedness theory

Coelho & Purkis (2009) highlight that the central challenge to the preparedness model is in the identification and discrimination of what is considered a prepared fear. For example, as we have already discussed, fear of spiders is often referred to as 'biologically prepared' or fear-relevant. However, only a very small proportion of spiders worldwide are venomous. They compare this to the number of poisonous mushrooms; there are, citing approximately, 100 poisonous species in the United States alone (Lincoff & Mitchell, 1977) posing a greater evolutionary threat to humans than snakes and spiders combined (Delprato, 1980). For more discussion of the preparedness theory and spider phobia, see Box 3.5.

The non-associative model: An alternative account of being biologically 'prepared' for fear

In the preceding section, we discussed evidence for the preparedness theory. This theory assumes that certain stimuli have the evolutionary potential to be associated with fear. However, this model does not predict that a fear response would be evident on first contact with a 'prepared' stimulus, for example, water. Associative learning (by conditioning, vicarious learning or information) is still required at some point of the species' and organisms' learning history, but with a relevant match between conditioned stimulus and unconditioned stimulus for fear acquisition. More recently, researchers have proposed a 'non-associative' model, arguing that conditioning events are not required for the onset of fear responses to stimuli that have evolutionary significance (fear-relevant stimuli) (e.g., Poulton & Menzies, 2002b). 'Non-associative' theorists contend that people are born with innate fears of fear-relevant stimuli (such as water, heights and snakes) and that what they learn is to overcome these existing predispositions. Support for this theory comes from studies which have shown that many phobics consider their fears started after their first contact with the stimulus. Menzies & Clarke (1993b) use the example of water phobia. They reported that only one of fifty parents identified a classical conditioning episode to explain their child's water phobia, and there was also lack of support for vicarious learning or the role of information. Adding some weight to this theory, Graham & Gaffan (1997) investigated children with or without a water phobia and concluded that the groups did not differ in the incidence of negative experiences with water. According to the mothers, seven out of the nine children with water phobia had shown fear since their first contact.

The non-associative model also recognises that a number of common specific phobias, such as dental phobia, are unlikely to have a basis in evolution. This model integrates the **associative model** (conditioning) to account for fears with no evolutionary basis, stating that conditioning experiences are needed to acquire a fear that is not evolutionarily relevant. To illustrate this, Poulton et al. (1997) explored the relationship between conditioning experiences and fear through the severity of teeth caries in a **prospective study**. They found that caries experience at age 5 was not related to the development of dental fear in late adolescence. In contrast, caries experience at age 15 was significantly, and specifically, related to the report of dental fear (but not other fears) at age 18. The authors suggest that poor dental health that requires a more demanding treatment increases the likelihood of aversive conditioning and seems to have a causal relationship with fear of dental treatment situations at age 18. This is seen to be consistent with the conditioning theory and also with the non-associative model, that is, conditioning explains the acquisition of fear as dentists and dental treatment do not represent an old evolutionary threat.

Box 3.6: Latent inhibition

Latent inhibition in fear acquisition refers to the idea that if an individual has a number of good experiences with a stimulus before they encounter a traumatic event, then they will be less likely to acquire a fear. Davey (1989) asked 101 students about their dental experiences and attitudes to dental care. Participants were divided into four groups depending on how their attitude to dental treatment had changed since they started receiving dental treatment. They were: (1) Always been anxious about dental treatment (A), (2) Once anxious but now relaxed (A»R), (3) Once relaxed but now anxious (R»A) and (4) Never been anxious (R).

Although 93 per cent of anxious participants had suffered at least one painful experience, 60 per cent of group R had had at least one painful experience and had gone on to be relaxed with dental treatment. This is inconsistent with the traditional conditioning accounts. The mean age of the first dental treatment for all the groups was 4–5 years. However, the first painful treatment of group R was between 12 and 13 years, and between 9 and 10 years in groups A and A»R. Therefore group R participants had their first painful treatment significantly later. Davey reports that in conditioning terms, this illustrates latent inhibition, and means that the continuous 2–3 years of good experience would discount the later traumatic experience. The conditions that foster 'latent inhibition' result either in the delayed acquisition of an association between a conditioned stimulus and unconditioned stimulus or no conditioning at all.

Points for discussion:

Does latent inhibition help explain why some people go on to develop a fear and others don't?

How might Davey's study suffer from some of the same methodological limitations as have been well documented for conditioning studies?

De Jongh et al. (1995) argue there might be 'a chicken and an egg' situation in these type of studies. That is, the anxious participants consider themselves anxious leading them to perceive their earlier dental treatments as painful and traumatic. To what extent do you consider this to be relevant?

Criticisms of the 'non-associative' account for specific phobia acquisition

There has been much criticism of the non-associative account of phobia acquisition, most notably from Mineka & Öhman (2002). They criticise the fact that Poulton & Menzies use the absence of conditioning episodes for evolutionary-relevant phobias, based on the self-report retrospective recall literature, as evidence for their theory. They argue that this is an 'awkward claim' (p. 174) and point out that studies that have compared rates of traumatic direct or indirect conditioning histories in phobics/non-phobics and found no differences are completely inconclusive.

Mineka & Öhman (2002) criticise the non-associative theory on other counts; we have already covered some of these when discussing method-ological limitations in retrospective recall (and they are widely docu-mented). Most notably, they focus on the major shortcomings of relying on retrospective recall especially when it may be a long period of time after the traumatic event took place. In addition, Coelho & Purkis (2009) have questioned the way that Menzies & Clarke (1993a) have assessed the origins of phobias. They argue that allowing a response choice such as 'I was always this way' reinforces the non-associative account. Moreover, response options such as 'I don't know / remember how I became phobic' does not necessarily support the non-associative account, rather it may be more reflective of problems relating to self-report and memory. The style of questioning exaggerates estimates of non-associative aetiology (Muris et al., 2002).

Related to their criticisms of the non-associative account, Mineka & Öhman (2002) make a number of pertinent points regarding **individual difference variables** in relation to why only some people who undergo a traumatic event develop a phobia. They argue that often researchers neglect to include any measure of individual difference variables that might account for (individually or in combination with other variables) why some individuals undergoing a trauma developed a phobia. They include within this variables such as whether someone has control over a traumatic event (which we covered in more detail when we discussed cognitive explanations) with far less fear being conditioned for an aver-sive event when it is controllable than when it is uncontrollable (e.g. Craske et al., 1990; Mineka et al., 1984). Moreover, although it appears counterintuitive it seems likely that non-fearful individuals would experi-ence more traumatic events simply because they are more likely to engage with the stimulus thus have more opportunities for possible traumas. For example, the snake phobic who avoids snakes at all times is much less likely to be bitten by one than individuals who like snakes and interact with them regularly. Yet because the non-fearful individual probably has a history of positive experiences with snakes, if they did get bitten by one, they are probably less likely to acquire a fear. This may be through the process known as latent inhibition (see Box 3.6). Therefore, it is probably not surprising that studies such as the ones that are cited by Menzies and colleagues have reported that non-fearful individuals recall more negative experiences because they have had more opportunities to have experienced them.

The fear module theory

Related to the notion of evolutionary threat, Öhman & Mineka (2001) proposed that there is an evolved fear module – a neural system that is selectively sensitive to evolutionarily relevant threat stimuli. Individuals who are quicker at detecting evolutionary threats (such as snakes and spiders) would have been more likely to escape them and hence to survive, reproduce and pass on their genes. Within this theoretical view it is proposed that the **amygdala** operates primarily as a rapid-response 'fear module' in the brain that enables both the perception of fear in others and the experience of fear within the individual. Such an evolved fear module is assumed to have been shaped and constrained by evolution so that it is preferentially activated within aversive contexts by stimuli that are relevant in a **phylogenetic** sense. However, Öhman & Mineka (2001) also state that threat-relevant stimuli with a strong **ontogenetic** history (e.g., guns) can also gain access to the fear module, however they should be able to activate this system to a lesser degree so that only mildly aversive 'prepared' stimuli may evoke a strong fear response (Öhman & Mineka, 2001). In other words, the fear module, with the **amygdala** at its centre, is considered to be more easily accessed by threat-related stimuli that have a fear-relevant evolutionary history.

Supporting evidence for the rapid detection of evolutionarily relevant threat stimuli has been shown from visual search studies showing faster detection of fear-relevant than fear-irrelevant stimuli. For example, LoBue & DeLoache (2008) found that both adults and children could detect images of snakes among a variety of non-threatening objects more quickly than they could pinpoint frogs, flowers or caterpillars. This finding has also been replicated in a study by Fox et al. (2007). However, Fox and colleagues also used the visual search task to test whether **phylogenetically** fear-relevant stimuli (snakes) were detected more efficiently (as would be predicted by the fear module theory) than **ontogenetically** (guns) fear-relevant stimuli. Results showed that the modern threat (guns) was detected as efficiently as the more ancient threat (snakes). The authors conclude that although the present results cannot be taken as evidence against the notion of an evolved fear module, they are broadly consistent with the notion that it is whether the threat is *appraised as relevant* that influences whether it is detected more efficiently.

Purkis & Lipp (2007) have shown that although snakes and spiders are preferentially attended to, negative evaluations are not automatically elicited during this processing. In their study, they compared the responses to stimuli of participants with no particular experience with snakes and spiders, to those of snake and spider experts. They showed that although all participants preferentially attended to snakes or spiders, only inexperienced participants displayed a negative response. Thus the study showed a clear difference between preferential attention and the accompanying emotional response: that is, you can preferentially attend to a stimulus without a negative emotional response being elicited. The authors contend that their findings are 'inconsistent with the idea of an automatic and negative response to fear-relevant stimuli' (p. 322).

Section summary

There have been a number of biological explanations proposed to explain why some people develop a specific phobia, including recent twin research concerning the role of genetics. It is clear that this type of methodology has the potential to provide clarity on the genetic link in specific phobia. We have also discussed theories supporting the role of evolution – that we are more 'prepared' to be fearful of certain stimuli that pose danger, and that through evolution we have developed a fear module – a neural system that is selectively sensitive to relevant threat stimuli. There is certainly research evidence to support such an evolutionary basis; however, findings are far from conclusive and there has been 'hot debate' on the methodological problems in some bodies of research.

Chapter summary

In this chapter, we have explored the different psychological and biological theories, and explanations that have been proposed for why phobias develop. There has been a great deal of empirical work conducted to provide evidence for these models and as a result we have a large body of research to inform our understanding of phobia development. However, more research is necessary to fully understand the aetiology of this phobic disorder. For example, after years of research on conditioning models there is still controversy as to the pathways to phobia development.

Newer perspectives have contributed to the debate on phobia aetiology and have also created more methodologically rigorous study designs and comprehensive paradigms, rather than continuing to fall back on methodology which has been shown time and again to be limited and at times flawed (e.g., retrospective recall in already anxious adults). This is encouraging. In the next chapter we turn our attention to how specific phobias can be treated, drawing on many of the theories and explanations we have covered here.

◉ Further reading

Armfield, J.M. (2006) Cognitive vulnerability: A model of the etiology of fear. *Clincal Psychology Review*, 26, 746–768.

Askew, C. & Field, A.P. (2007) Vicarious learning and the development of fears in childhood. *Behaviour Research and Therapy*, 45, 2616–2627.

Beck, A.T. & Emery, G. (1985) *Anxiety Disorders and Phobias: A Cognitive Perspective*. New York: Basic Books.

Key search terms

Classical conditioning; latent inhibition, preparedness, vicarious learning, cognitive vulnerability model, fear module theory.

Chapter 4

Specific phobia: Treatment

👁 Introduction

In Chapter 3 we considered the different explanations and theories that have been proposed for why some individuals develop specific phobias (and importantly why others don't). In this chapter, we turn our attention to the different types of treatments for specific phobias.

> **In this chapter, we will:**
> - Consider why individuals with specific phobia rarely seek treatment
> - Consider how treatment outcome is assessed in specific phobia
> - Describe the different treatments available for specific phobia
> - Discuss the evidence for different treatments for specific phobia
> - Consider the limitations of treatment studies in specific phobia and future directions

Treatments for specific phobia: Key issues

Before we discuss the different types of treatments available for specific phobia, there are some important issues to consider in order to put these treatments in context. We consider some of these below.

Presenting for treatment and treatment efficacy: A dichotomy

There are clear dichotomies when it comes to treatment for specific phobias. Firstly, although specific phobias are the most prevalent of the phobic disorders (indeed all anxiety disorders), it is well-known that individuals rarely seek treatment (Regier et al., 1993). Secondly, specific phobia is considered one of the success stores in the field of treatment and is often seen as a 'solved problem'. This is well illustrated by Wolitzky-Taylor et al. (2008) who conducted a **meta-analysis** which included 33 **randomised controlled trials** (RCTs) investigating psychological treatments for specific phobia. They found that the average participant receiving treatment was better off than approximately 85 per cent of participants who did not receive treatment.

Why do individuals with specific phobia not seek treatment?

If treatments have been shown to be effective why do sufferers not seek treatment? Wolitzky-Taylor and colleagues (2008) summarise some of the most common explanations. First, many phobic individuals perceive their phobia as untreatable, or are unaware of effective and available treatments. Second, as many of the available treatments involve direct exposure to the phobic stimulus, those who are aware of the available treatments may be apprehensive about engaging in them. Approximately 25 per cent of phobic patients refuse exposure-based treatment due to fear of facing the feared object or situation (Marks & O'Sullivan, 1988). This is further illustrated by Mandy's views on treatment for her spider phobia in Box 4.3 further on in this chapter. Third, some phobic individuals may be able to successfully avoid their feared target with little impact on their daily lives, which acts as a disincentive for seeking treatment. Finally, some individuals may have experienced a failure in conducting self-administered exposure and have therefore concluded that they are unresponsive to this mode of treatment.

How do we assess the effectiveness of different treatments?

Before we consider the variety and nature of treatments available for specific phobias, it is important to consider how researchers and clinicians determine the efficacy of such treatments. In other words, how do they assess (1) whether a treatment is successful and (2) to what extent it is successful? We considered many of the measures used to assess treatment efficacy in detail in Chapter 2 when we discussed how specific phobia can be measured. The main measure employed in studies to determine treatment efficacy is a BAT. A BAT comprises a series of tasks in which the participant is observed approaching the feared object or situation. As we can see from Box 4.1 the tasks are graded (so entering the dental room is step 1 and actually being able to have a cavity filled is the final step at 14). The advantages of a BAT are that it is objective and visible – the researcher or clinician can actually 'see' how the participant is responding to the stimulus and what stage they are able to get to in terms of confronting the stimulus (e.g., only able to enter the dental room). Self-report measures are also employed regularly to assess important indicators such as anxiety levels, beliefs and daily function. These complement BATs because achievements in a BAT do not necessarily reflect what Choy et al. (2007) refer to as 'real life gains'. However, the downside of self-report is that it is (by its very nature) subjective, and it is easier to 'fake'. Thus studies often use both BATs and self-report in order to provide a comprehensive measure of treatment efficacy.

Outcome measures: A word of caution

Choy et al. (2007) note that a statistically significant change on a BAT or a self-report questionnaire does not necessarily reflect *clinically significant improvement*. There are many different definitions of what a 'clinically significant improvement' might be (e.g., that a score in the range of a dysfunctional population at pre-treatment should fall within the range of a normal population after treatment (Jacobson et al., 1984)). The important point to make here is that it shouldn't just be that participants fare better after treatment (and/or compared to controls) but that they should be reporting and displaying scores that indicate *a clinical improvement in terms of their specific phobia*.

Box 4.1: Steps in behaviour avoidance test: An example for dental phobia

Haukebø et al. (2008) designed a test of behavioural avoidance for their study on one-session vs. five-session treatment for dental phobia. This test comprises operationalised steps, including some of the most usual procedures inherent in a routine dental appointment. The test is carried out by a dentist (who doesn't know which condition the participant is in), but the patient can discontinue at any point.

1. Enter dental treatment room
2. Sit down in treatment chair
3. Fasten paper bib round neck
4. Lower back of chair
5. Lower lamp towards patient's face
6. Put instrument table closer toward patient
7. Open the mouth
8. Clinical exam with mirror
9. Offer to drill and fill a cavity
10. Apply topical anaesthesia
11. Inject local anaesthesia
12. Apply saliva suction
13. Drill the cavity
14. Fill the cavity

👁 Psychological treatments

It is very clear that by far the most common way of treating specific phobias is by psychological means, thus we will mostly focus on these types of treatments. Within this section, we will consider some of the main psychological treatments that have been proposed, which are

- Exposure-based therapies
- Cognitive therapies
- Eye movement desensitisation and reprocessing (EMDR)

As the therapies that include an exposure element are the most common type of psychological therapy, we will begin by discussing these therapies in most detail.

👁 Exposure-based therapy

Background

The most generally accepted treatment of choice for specific phobia is exposure therapy, which has been shown to be very effective across a variety of treatment outcomes (Choy et al., 2007; Wolitzy-Taylor et al., 2008). Exposure-based therapies reflect a variety of behavioural approaches that are all based on exposing the individual to their phobic stimulus. Thus, these relate to the conditioning theories we covered in Chapter 3. From a behavioural perspective, specific phobias are maintained because of avoidance of the phobic stimulus, thus phobic individuals have no opportunity to learn

- that they can tolerate the fear
- that the fear will reduce on its own without them avoiding the stimulus or escaping from it
- what they fear will result from the interaction will not actually happen (e.g., that the dog will not attack them), or it won't be as awful as they imagine.

Since escaping from the phobic object reduces the individuals' anxiety, avoidance behaviour is reinforced (see Figure 4.1). Avoidance can occur by not entering a situation or avoiding the object of the fear. A dog phobic may avoid dogs and situations that may potentially involve dogs. As they do not put themselves in the position of interacting with dogs, they do not have the opportunity to let their anxiety subside and to realise that dogs normally do not attack, bite and so on (which may be the most feared situation). Alternatively, a phobic individual may enter the situation but may not experience it fully, for example, a flight phobic may drink alcohol or take some tranquillisers before flying; an individual who has a phobia of bridges may have someone hold their hand while they run across the bridge as fast as possible with their eyes closed and humming loudly (in order to 'zone out' of the experience).

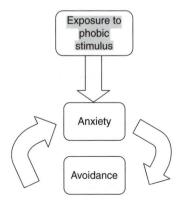

Figure 4.1 How anxiety is maintained by avoiding the feared stimulus

Exposure therapies are thus designed to encourage the individual to enter feared situations (either in reality or through imaginal exercises) and to try to remain in it. The graded situations typically follow an individually tailored 'fear hierarchy' or 'exposure hierarchy' that starts with situations that are only mildly anxiety-provoking to the individual and builds up to those that are feared the most. See Box 4.2 for Mandy's individual fear hierarchy for her spider phobia (you will remember Mandy from Chapters 2 and 3). Note that another individual's fear hierarchy may look different to this; for example, the drawings/photos may not induce any anxiety, so they may not be included, but there may be more steps further up the hierarchy ladder that are not included in Mandy's.

Flooding/Implosion therapy: Putting the most-feared situation first

It is worth noting that there are some forms of exposure therapy (e.g., implosion therapy or flooding) that turn this premise on its head; that is the individual is exposed to the most anxiety-provoking stimulus straight away and is required to stay in that situation. For example, Mandy would be required to start at the top of her fear hierarchy and hold the spider straightaway and continue holding it; this is based on the idea that you can't stay anxious indefinitely. If the phobic individual can bear it, at the end of it they may well be able to see that they have survived unharmed and the basis of their phobia is unfounded. This technique should be supervised by a trained therapist and it, unsurprisingly, requires a very-motivated patient. The extreme discomfort implicit in this method tends to discourage its wide use.

Box 4.2: Mandy's fear hierarchy

1 Think about a spider;
2 Look at a cartoon drawing of a spider;
3 Look at a serious drawing of a spider;
4 Look at a photo of a spider;
5 Look at an empty spider web;
6 Touch an empty spider web;

7 Look at a real spider in a box;
8 Hold the box with the spider;
9 Look at a real spider, not in a box, from across the room;
10 Look at a real spider from halfway across the room;
11 Look at a real spider up close;
12 Let a spider crawl on something I'm holding (e.g., a piece of paper);
13 Hold a spider in my hand.

In vivo exposure

In vivo exposure involves actually confronting the feared stimuli, usually in a graduated fashion. At first, a hierarchy of concerns about the phobia is established starting with the most-feared aspects and going to the least-feared aspects (see Box 4.2). Exposure then occurs, first to the less-feared aspect until no anxiety is experienced, followed by exposure to the next feared aspect in the hierarchy. In time, less anxiety occurs in the phobic situation, a phenomenon known as habituation. The treatment usually lasts a number of hours, and can be administered in one very-long session (e.g., one 3-hour session) or across multiple sessions (e.g., three to eight 1–1.5-hour-long sessions).

Choy et al. (2007), in their review of different treatments for specific phobia, found *in vivo* exposure to be the most robust treatment for the specific phobia types, with most studies finding it more effective than placebo or **wait-list control**, and some studies providing success rates in the range of 80–90 per cent. The authors also found that treatment gains of *in vivo* exposure were either maintained or improved further over time (these include studies on animal phobias, heights and claustrophobia). The efficacy of *in vivo* exposure was supported by a **meta-analysis** of 33 randomised treatment studies (Wolitzky-Taylor et al., 2008), where it was found to outperform alternative modes of exposure (e.g., imaginal exposure, virtual reality, etc.; see below for discussion of these) at post-treatment. Interestingly, this benefit was not evident at follow-up. However, this was not because the *in vivo* group had a greater return of their fear, rather it was due to those in the alternative modes of exposure groups continuing to improve post-treatment. Why should this be the case? Wolitzky-Taylor and colleagues put forward several plausible explanations. First, they suggest that the lack of significant differences at follow-up may be due to continued naturalistic exposure during the post-treatment to follow-up period. That is, those who received the alternative modes of exposure therapy may have engaged with their phobic stimulus more than the *in vivo* participants between the time they finished the therapeutic intervention and the time they were followed-up. For example, a dog phobic may have put themselves in situations where they would have to interact with dogs, or they might not have gone out of their way to avoid situations where they would have to be around dogs. However, none of the studies in their review reported data on this (we go on to discuss this problem further on in the chapter), so this can't be confirmed. Second, Wolitzky-Taylor and colleagues suggest that there may be a **ceiling effect** for the participants who took part in the *in vivo* exposure. Even though those receiving non-*in-vivo* exposure continued to improve from post to follow-up, their fear reduction did not surpass that of those receiving *in vivo* exposure, thus perhaps the reduction in fear for the *in vivo* participants was so high post-treatment there was little room for improvement.

Wolitzky-Taylor and colleagues claim that these two possibilities may not be mutually exclusive. Improvement for those in the *in vivo* exposure conditions may have reached a **ceiling effect**, while those receiving non-*in-vivo* exposure treatments may have had more room for improvement, which they achieved via naturalistic exposure from the post to follow-up periods. Thus, it is important for future studies to include the level of self-exposure to the phobic stimulus in order to disentangle these effects. We briefly discuss this later on in the chapter when we consider the factors that might influence treatment outcome.

Systematic desensitisation and imaginal exposure

In the late 1950s Joseph Wolpe developed a treatment programme for anxiety that was based on the principles of classical conditioning. Wolpe found that anxiety symptoms could be reduced (or inhibited) when exposing fearful individuals to their phobic stimulus (via fear-evoking images and thoughts – known as imaginal exposure – or sometimes to the actual phobic stimulus itself) in a graded order and systematically paired with a relaxation response. By substituting a new response to a feared situation (a trained contradictory response of relaxation which is irreconcilable with an anxious response) phobic reactions are diminished or eradicated. Hence this process of reciprocal inhibition came to be called *systematic desensitisation*.

Systematic desensitisation essentially comprises three procedures. First, the patient is trained in progressive muscular relaxation (for details see Box 4.3). After learning relaxation skills, the client and therapist create a hierarchy of stimulus situations ranging from those that trigger very low levels of anxiety (e.g., imagining a cartoon drawing of a spider) to the one that elicits the phobic reaction (e.g., creating a vivid image of holding a spider). With the therapist's support and assistance (and usually while remaining in the therapist's office), the patient proceeds through the anxiety hierarchy, responding to the presentation of each fearful image by producing the state of relaxation. The patient stays with each step until a relaxed state is reliably produced when faced with each item. As tolerance develops for each identified item in the series, the individual moves on to the next. In facing more fear-provoking images progressively, and developing a consistent pairing of relaxation with the feared object, relaxation rather than anxiety becomes associated with the source of their anxiety. Thus, a gradual desensitisation occurs, with relaxation replacing anxiety and fear.

Treatment using systematic desensitisation tends to take longer than *in vivo* exposure, and appears to be more effective at changing subjective anxiety than at reducing avoidance of the phobic stimulus (e.g., individuals may still go out of their way to avoid situations where they may come into contact with a spider). Thus, it is not recommended as the first choice of treatment if the phobic individual is willing to try *in vivo* or an alternative form of exposure therapy. Systematic desensitisation is primarily used in treatment for those disorders for which exposure-based treatments are not appropriate. For example, it can be used when the patient is unable or unwilling to be exposed to their actual phobic stimuli, or when exposure is unfeasible (e.g., it is not always easy for therapists to lay their hands on a snake or to facilitate a flight) and it can be used as the first step towards exposure treatment.

Box 4.3: What is involved in progressive relaxation?

In progressive relaxation, one first tightens and then relaxes various muscle groups in the body. During the alternating clenching and relaxing, the client should be focusing on the contrast between the initial tension and the subsequent feelings of relaxation and softening that develop once the tightened muscles are released. After discovering how muscles feel when they are deeply relaxed, repeated practice enables a person to recreate the relaxed sensation intentionally in a variety of situations.

Virtual reality

In recent years, researchers have applied virtual reality (VR) technology to the treatment of specific phobias. VR has been mostly employed as a tool for exposure therapy, called VR exposure therapy (VRET), and has been primarily used to provide systematic exposure to anxiety-provoking cues via computer-generated environments, thus it becomes a computer-based alternative to standard *in vivo* exposure (Powers & Emmelkamp, 2008). These treatments involve exposing patients to their feared stimuli using computer-generated, interactive, virtual environments that the clinician or patient can manipulate. Most recently, it has gained a great deal of attention in the treatment of height and flying phobia. It uses computer-generated environments to simulate stimuli through multiple sensorial channels (mainly visual and auditory), thereby allowing the user to interact with the virtual world while also achieving a sense of being physically there (Tortella-Feliu et al., 2011).

Evidence supports that VRET is effective at treating anxiety disorders, as recently summarised in the **meta-analytic** studies of Powers & Emmelkamp (2008), and Wolitzky-Taylor et al. (2008). Moreover, Choy et al. (2007) found that VR treatment could be as effective as *in vivo* exposure for flying and height phobia, and more effective than systematic desensitisation. It has also enhanced the effects of cognitive therapy for flying phobia (Mühlberger et al., 2003). However, Choy and colleagues call for larger controlled studies in order to provide further support for this mode of treatment for flying and height phobia.

What are the advantages of VR?

There a number of advantages of VR exposure therapy which have been highlighted in the literature (Coelho et al., 2009; Tortella-Feliu et al., 2011). First, for phobic stimuli that are difficult to reproduce in real life (e.g., flying, thunderstorms, being on top of very high building) VR treatments are likely to provide a valuable alternative to traditional *in vivo* procedures. Second, when using a VR system the therapist and patient do not need to leave the consulting room. This indicates the saving of time and money. Moreover, it may save the patient from being embarrassed publicly (e.g., becoming very anxious on a flight) as well as preserving their confidentiality. Patients may feel more secure during sessions, and there is a higher level of control of the exposure conditions, which is important in practice, as well as for research studies.

VR can be either an intermediate step towards live exposure (i.e., getting on a plane, standing on top of a very high building), as an end in itself or an alternative for those phobic individuals who have difficulty with imaginal exposure. Indeed by creating stimuli of lesser magnitude than is experienced in the real world, patients may start treatment even if they are too fearful to be exposed to 'the real thing'. However, Choy et al. (2007) note that in contrast to flying phobia, the cost-effectiveness of VR treatment for spider phobia is questionable given the ease of obtaining a spider for *in vivo* exposure!

What factors are important in exposure-based therapy?

There have been a number of studies that have sought to understand the factors that might impact upon the effectiveness of exposure-based treatments for specific phobia, including the frequency of exposure sessions, the context of exposure practices, the number of sessions and the therapeutic relationship/level of involvement. Let's consider these briefly.

Number of sessions

There has been some debate regarding the number of sessions needed for exposure therapy to be effective. Wolitzky-Taylor et al. (2008) recently found that contrary to the assertion that one session of exposure treatment is as effective as multiple sessions, multiple exposure sessions are more effective than one session of exposure particularly at follow-up and suggest that clinicians should deliver treatment in multiple sessions to enhance long-term treatment gains. We discuss in more detail the one-session treatment (OST), which is a variant of exposure therapy a bit later in the chapter.

The therapist: Trust and level of involvement matter

If someone is very afraid of something, he or she will usually not want to confront it. The patient must trust that the clinician has the patient's safety in mind, and will not expose the patient to any real harm. Further, clinicians should ensure that they do not introduce more fear-evoking stimuli until the patient's anxiety has been significantly reduced with the less-extreme stimuli. For example, if the patient still demonstrates extreme anxiety when viewing a video of a snake, he or she isn't ready to be brought into contact with a real, live snake.

The level of involvement of the therapist can also be important. Öst et al. (1991) compared spider phobic individuals who had either a single session of therapist-assisted exposure therapy or self-directed exposure via a self-help manual. Findings showed that the therapist-directed exposure performed significantly better than the self-directed exposure at reducing fear on self-report ratings, behavioural measures and clinician ratings (Öst et al., 1991). However, it can also make a difference where the self-directed exposure occurs, self-directed exposure in the clinic has been found to outperform self-directed exposures completed at home (Hellström & Öst, 1995).

Do advances in technology indicate less therapist involvement? Certainly, recent research has shown that computer-guided self-exposure can work just as well as therapist-guided exposure, at least in the short-term (Marks et al., 2004). For now, Grös & Antony (2006) suggest that newer technologies (e.g., Virtual Reality) may be used to administer the routine aspects of exposure therapy, thus saving clinician's valuable time and resources.

Can varying context influence outcome?

Varying the context of exposure (e.g., confronting dogs in several different places), as well as varying the stimuli used during practices (e.g., confronting a variety of different dogs), may lead to better outcomes, particularly over the long-term. Choy et al. (2007) reviewed three studies which partially support this notion. The first study (Rodriguez et al., 1999) did not find any significant difference in response between the groups tested in the original or novel context, but two later studies (Mineka et al., 1999; Mystkowski et al., 2002) did, after modifying the novel context to be more distinct from the original treatment context.

Have participants been receiving additional treatment during the follow-up period?

A potentially important issue that can affect outcome data is whether the participant has received additional treatment (even if it is self-administered). When participants are encouraged to continue self-exposure, there are positive results (Hellström & Öst, 1995; Hellström et al., 1996), suggesting that self-exposure is important in maintaining treatment gains. However, many studies do not record or report this data (Wolitzky-Taylor et al., 2008), as we discussed earlier. Wolitzky-Taylor and colleagues highlight this as an important issue for future research.

One-session treatment (OST)

As we have seen, there are many variants of empirically supported, exposure-based treatment. One variant, however, is unique in its combination of techniques over a single session. One-session treatment (OST) is a massed (lengthy) exposure therapy which lasts for usually a maximum of 3 hours over a single session. It is a **cognitive behavioural treatment** for specific phobia, which has prompted a large body of research in the last decade or so. Throughout the session, a therapist and client collaboratively work through the steps of the client's fear hierarchy. This differs from traditional *in vivo* exposure in that clients are gradually exposed to their entire fear hierarchy during the one single session. Zlomke & Davis (2008) provide a detailed description of OST as well as a review of treatment efficacy. They explain that the exposure component of OST is different from that of typical *in vivo* procedures; instead of progressing through a linear formal hierarchy, the *in vivo* part of OST progresses as a series of behavioural experiments. During the experiments the therapist is actively involved by, for example, prompting the client for their **catastrophic cognitions** and tries to guide them to more-rational conclusions. The therapist may also be involved in what is known as 'modelling'. That is, the therapist models appropriate interactions with the stimulus at each step. This is not only instructive for the client to successfully interact with the stimulus, but also serves as another level of exposure. Seeing a trusted person interact with a feared stimulus without negative consequence provides more evidence against the **catastrophic cognitions.**

Maintaining the effects of OST outwith the single session

An important feature of OST is that although it is conducted over one single session, this is just the start for the client. They are informed at the start that they must continue to expose themselves to their feared stimulus in their everyday lives for months post treatment to help maintain and stabilise treatment gains (Öst, 1989). As a result, OST is a therapy that requires a very-motivated client who will be asked to tolerate a reasonable amount of distress during the session and not attempt to escape or avoid interaction with the phobic stimulus as a result. OST sessions typically end when a predetermined goal is met (e.g., holding a spider) and the client's anxiety as well as belief in the catastrophic cognition has considerably decreased, ideally to zero.

Keeping the client 'in the dark': An ethical question for OST

Zlomke & Davis (2008) raise an important ethical question regarding OST, notably the lack of full disclosure about the treatment process. This surrounds one of the key goals of OST – the concept of overlearning. Overlearning is where the individual is encouraged to interact with the phobic stimulus at a level way beyond that which they would do in a natural environment. For example, for a snake phobic it would not just involve being able to look at a live snake, or to touch it briefly with one's hand. Overlearning may involve having several snakes draped over the client's neck. Similarly, for a spider phobic the overlearning aspect may not involve simply holding or touching a spider but having a large one crawl around in the client's hair over a prolonged period of time. The therapist's goal is to allow as much overlearning as possible. Öst (1997, 1989) suggested that not telling the client about the final goal of treatment helps them in completing the therapy successfully as worrying about this final stage would hinder earlier progress. Unsurprisingly, however, as many as 90 per cent of his adult clients would not have started or continued with OST had they known about the overlearning aspect beforehand. This is illustrated in the interview with Mandy, our spider-phobic (see Box 4.4). She is understandably shocked that this would occur in the session, and certainly wouldn't 'sign up for it'; however, she is reticent to confront her fear at all, and does concede that she understands why a therapist would do it. Nevertheless, this is an interesting ethical dilemma – one that prompts the following question: Does the end (successful treatment outcome) justify the means (not being completely truthful with the client at the start). You will no doubt have your own views on this!

Box 4.4: Case study: Mandy's views and experience of treatment

Mandy was interviewed by one of the authors (HB) regarding her views and experience on therapy for her spider phobia. Her thoughts are quite typical of individuals with specific phobias, and demonstrate some of the challenges of treating people with this type of phobia.

Mandy: 'I have never had therapy but I have considered it. I haven't gone through with it because I know that part of the treatment will involve facing my fear and I just can't bear to participate in something which I know will put me in that situation. On TV it always has the person having a tarantula in the palm of their hands as final proof of them overcoming their fear, and I can't begin to sign up for that! I wouldn't even consider therapy involving virtual reality – fake spiders are enough to put me off'.

'One-session therapy does sound interesting as it seems like a "quick fix", although it would depend on how it was explained prior to signing up, as any indication of having to "face the fear" would deter me from considering it'. [HB describes it in more detail also including the "overlearning" aspect. That is, that the therapist would not explain in advance that the goal would be for her to interact with spiders in a way not typically expected in the natural environment, for example, having a large spider crawl in her hair]. 'IN MY HAIR?? F'n h*ll!! On one hand I say that is unethical and that I would kill them for doing that; on the other hand, I'm unlikely to sign up for any therapy knowing in advance that I'd need to face my fear, so understand why they would do it. But that is going too far!'

How effective is OST and what are the potential advantages?

There are several studies in the literature demonstrating the efficacy of OST. For example, Haukebø et al. (2008) recruited 40 dental phobic individuals and randomly allocated them to **wait-list control**, OST or a five-session exposure treatment. The authors included a 1-year follow-up. Both treatments were equally effective at reducing avoidance behaviour and changing cognitions during the feared situation (see Box 4.1 for details of the BAT employed in this study). Haukebø and colleagues conclude that both treatment conditions enable a return to ordinary dental treatment. Zlomke & Davis (2008) echo this, and based on their review they conclude that OST is generally found to be effective, although more research is needed to identify the mechanism(s) through which the treatment produces effects. They make the final point that pragmatic and financial considerations should be taken into account for OST; although studies such as Haukebø et al.'s did not show superior treatment gains for the OST group over the five-session group, they did demonstrate equivalence (mirroring findings on claustrophobia; Öst et al., 2001). Thus shorter duration of treatment would result in less financial costs as well as less disruption to the client's life and schedule. These are important factors to consider, especially in times of austerity with efficiency and cost-effectiveness at a premium.

Section summary

Exposure therapy has been shown to be very effective for individuals with specific phobia. Generally, the research evidence does provide more substantial support for some exposure therapies (i.e., *in vivo* exposure) over others (e.g., systematic desensitisation) though there is debate as to whether long-term gains are maintained. If a patient lacks the motivation or courage to complete exposures, other psychological treatments may provide a suitable alternative. Let's consider what these alternatives might involve, and importantly, how effective they are in treating specific phobia.

👁 Non-exposure-based therapy

Cognitive therapy

Cognitive factors are considered an important component of anxiety as we saw in Chapter 3. Although cognitive therapy has been widely used and researched as a form of treatment for anxiety disorders in general, it was used less often in the treatment of specific phobias until recently. The ultimate goal of cognitive therapy is to modify distorted thoughts or misconceptions that are associated with the feared situation/object. The theory is that modifying these thoughts will result in a decrease in anxiety and avoidance. However, it is considered most effective when the patient fears what will *result* from being in the situation, rather than the situation itself, for example, where a flying phobic fears a plane crash, or a claustrophobic believes that the lift will break down and that there will be no oxygen left. Cognitive therapists would present the flying phobic with the statistical figures on plane crashes to help them re-evaluate the likelihood of a plane crash, and present the claustrophobic with information regarding how rare lift breakdowns are and that realistically they are more likely to fight for air if they took the alternative 30 flights of stairs option.

Cognitive therapy has been studied both as a solo treatment and as an **adjunctive therapy**. Choy et al. (2007) found that there is strong evidence supporting this type of therapy for the treatment of claustrophobia both on its own and as an adjunct to *in vivo* exposure. They contend that for claustrophobia cognitive therapy may be a good alternative to *in vivo* exposure. On its own, there is some evidence that cognitive therapy is effective for dental and flying phobia, but there appears to be not much added benefit from cognitive therapy as an adjunct to *in vivo* treatment for animal or flying phobia.

Eye movement desensitisation and reprocessing (EMDR)

EMDR is a relatively new technique that was originally proposed as a treatment method for **post-traumatic stress disorder**. EMDR involves repeated and lengthy imagined confrontations with phobic stimuli (e.g., imagining a snake) while an external distracting stimulus is alternated bilaterally. In most studies, the external stimulus is the therapist's finger moving back and forth across the patient's visual field while the patient tracks the movement of the finger. However, some practitioners use other visual stimuli (e.g., a moving light), auditory stimuli (e.g., tones presented to alternating ears), or tactile stimuli (e.g., tapping using alternating hands). The idea is that through eye movements, negative memories are emotionally processed and taken on board.

In a review of the existing research on anxiety disorders (including specific phobias) De Jongh & ten Broeke (2009) note that it is disappointing to find that 20 years after its introduction, support for the efficacy of EMDR is still scarce. Although this may be due to methodological limitations in some of the studies, it is also possible that EMDR may not be consistently effective in specific phobias. De Jongh et al. (1999) suggest that since EMDR is a treatment for distressing memories and related pathologies, it may be most effective in treating specific phobias which follow a traumatic experience (e.g., dog phobia after a dog bite), and less effective for those of unknown onset (e.g., when a person has no recollection of how they acquired their dog phobia). It has also been suggested that the active component of EMDR is the imaginal exposure; indeed Sanderson & Carpenter (1992) highlight that research has shown that the imaginal exposure used during EMDR is just as effective regardless of whether the eye movements are included or not.

Overall, findings from the review by De Jongh & ten Broeke (2009) suggest that EMDR is generally more effective than no-treatment control conditions or non-specific interventions but less effective than existing evidence-based (i.e., exposure-based) interventions. However, an advantage of EMDR is that it can be used in cases for which *in vivo* exposure is difficult to administer, for example for phobias that are limited to events, for example thunderstorms, or when it is logistically difficult to acquire the phobic stimulus, for example rare animals (De Jongh et al., 1999).

◉ Biological treatments

Medication in the treatment of specific phobia: The road less travelled

Unlike other anxiety disorders, few studies have evaluated the efficacy of pharmacological approaches, and no drug has yet been approved for the treatment of specific phobia. The general view is that medication has limited utility (e.g., Harvey & Rapee, 2002). Choy et al. (2007) review the evidence and conclude that there are some limited data to suggest that **benzodiazepines** may be helpful in acute situations, such as for enabling a flight phobic to complete a flight or a dental phobic to undergo a dental procedure. However, the anxiety returns without medication. Thus, although benzodiazepines might inhibit subjective fear during phobic confrontation, they do not increase approach behaviour. Some have argued that **benzodiazepines** might even be harmful in that they create state dependency effects. That is, phobic individuals learn to approach the phobic stimulus when 'drugged', but this learning is not transferred to a non-drugged state. Indeed, it has been recommended to commissioners of UK clinical psychology services in dentistry that specialist psychological treatment approaches would be a more appropriate alternative for dental phobic individuals, with the added benefit that patients can learn to manage their fear and change previous patterns of behaviour (Hainsworth & Buchanan, 2009).

Applied muscle tension: A unique treatment for blood-injury-injection phobia

In Chapter 2 we discussed B-I-I and its unique characteristics (see Box 2.1). That is, most B-I-I patients have a biphasic physiological response to their phobic stimulus (blood, needles, etc.). This **biphasic reaction** involves blood pressure and heart rate first rising (as in normal anxiety) and then rapidly dropping, leading to fainting. Drawing upon this response, an applied muscle tension method was devised. This involves teaching patients to tense the muscles of the body in order to increase blood pressure and reduce the likelihood of fainting when phobic stimuli are encountered. Choy et al. (2007) found that two controlled studies provided sound evidence of its use and that there is some supporting evidence for long-term efficacy at 12-months follow-up based on a BAT (watching a bloody scene in a film; Öst et al., 1991) and it has been recommended as the treatment of choice for B-I-I patients (Grös & Antony, 2006).

Alternative ways for 'treating' individuals with specific phobia: The role of support groups

Support groups

As we have noted, individuals with a specific phobia do not generally present for treatment as they do not want to be faced with their feared stimulus (see Mandy's view of having therapy for her spider phobia in Box 4.4). There are some phobias that can be avoided relatively easily with no major impact on everyday life. For example, if you live in the UK you can probably avoid snakes fairly easily (though images do appear relatively frequently, via television, newspapers, etc.). However, as we discussed in Chapter 2, there are specific phobias such as dental phobia, which can have a detrimental effect on the life (and sometimes health) of the sufferer. Instead of 'professional' psychological therapy, these phobic individuals sometimes turn to support groups, which can provide an opportunity to share experiences and anxiety in a supportive environment and may ultimately lead to confrontation of the phobic stimulus. These support groups sometimes (though by no means always) involve a health professional. For example, Crawford et al. (1997) conducted an evaluation of a face-to-face support group for dentally anxious adults, who were avoiding dental care, with a dentist as group leader. The group was shown to be successful in various ways, including confidence building and ability to attend for dental treatment. However, some weaknesses were acknowledged, including inconvenience experienced through attendance at meetings over lunchtime and dependence on the dentist as a group leader.

Online support groups

With the growth of the Internet, there exist a growing number of online support groups for various conditions, illnesses and nowadays specific phobias. Commentators have established that there are a number of advantages of such groups (Coulson, 2005; White & Dorman, 2001; Winzelberg et al., 2002). First, they are not restricted by the temporal, geographical and spatial limitations typically associated with face-to-face groups, and so individuals can send and receive messages at any time of the day. Second, online support groups may bring together a more varied range of individuals offering diverse perspectives, experiences, opinions and sources of information than might otherwise be the case. Third, participation in an online support group allows a greater degree of anonymity than face-to-face groups. Such anonymity may facilitate self-disclosure and help individuals in discussing sensitive issues more easily or to give opinions with less fear of embarrassment or judgement than in more traditional face-to-face groups (Ferguson, 1997; Klemm & Nolan, 1998; Madara, 1997). These factors may be particularly relevant for phobic individuals.

Research in focus: Can Internet support groups help dental phobic individuals?

As we discussed in Chapter 2, having a dental phobia can negatively impact on the individual's life. With the growth in Internet support groups, and their many potential advantages (as outlined above), dentally anxious or phobic individuals may increasingly be choosing to access these groups. However, there is a lack of research considering the specific reasons why individuals may be accessing dental anxiety or phobia support groups and their experiences of accessing such groups. Moreover, little is known about how (or even if) they feel these groups are helping them with their anxiety. Therefore, Buchanan and Coulson conducted a series of studies in order to explore these questions using both qualitative and quantitative methods.

The authors posted an online questionnaire to the online support group forum Dental Fear Central (http://www.dentalfearcentral.org). Participants were asked for their own self-reported evaluation of the efficacy of the support group, and also to complete the Modified Dental Anxiety Scale (MDAS; see Chapter 2 for details). Findings showed that 60 per cent of the sample considered that the support group had 'somewhat' or 'greatly lessened' their anxiety. Overall MDAS scores were significantly lower in the 'greatly lessened' group (Coulson & Buchanan, 2007).

> **Box 4.5: Questions posed to participants taking part in a study exploring the nature of experiences of individuals accessing a dental anxiety online support group (Coulson & Buchanan, 2007)**
>
> In your own words, could you tell us why you decided to participate in an online support group?
>
> In your view, has being a member of an online support group made any difference to how you cope with your dental anxiety/phobia? If so, could you give some examples?
>
> What do you consider to be the main advantages of participating in an online support group?
>
> Are there any problems you have experienced in participating in an online support group?'

Participants were also asked open-ended questions (see Box 4.5) regarding the nature of their online experiences in relation to the forum, and responses were analysed qualitatively (Buchanan & Coulson, 2007). The emergent themes suggest that feeling less isolated, sharing experiences with others, giving and receiving information and advice, and becoming empowered were key functions, important consequences and meaningful experiences for the group. For example, the group appeared to have an immediate benefit in that participants no longer felt that they were alone in trying to cope with their dental anxiety or phobia but rather were now part of a larger community. The online group offered individuals a virtual meeting place through which they could communicate with others who have the same or similar problems. Of particular benefit to individuals was the empathy and understanding, which was offered by others who truly understood their fears and anxieties. For example, one participant wrote:

> Being able to find other caring and sympathetic people who know how you feel. Most people I talk to all say the same thing 'oh nobody likes going to the dentist'. They do not understand that this is not just a little nervousness, it is full blown fear. This support group has been a good place to come anytime I need reassurance (26-year-old female).

Through the support group, members were able to obtain rich and varied sources of emotional and informational support, which focused on the everyday realities of coping with dental anxiety or phobia. This advice included coping with the oral health implications (e.g., decaying teeth) and the psychosocial consequences of their fear (stigma, shame and embarrassment). Informational support often took the form of providing members with practical information, such as new treatment advances and contact details of supportive dentists. These findings are consistent with other studies which have suggested that emotional and informational support are often the most frequent types of social support given within online support groups (Brennan & Fink, 1997; Coulson, 2005; Preece, 2001).

These exploratory studies suggest that for most individuals accessing this online support group was a positive and beneficial experience. However, there are some of methodological issues which are raised by these studies and should be considered. Firstly, the participants may not be representative of all dentally anxious and phobic individuals who use Internet support groups as the invitation to participate was posted on only one board. Secondly, it may be the case that only those who held a positive view of the group chose to participate. Third, in the absence of any baseline measures of dental anxiety (prior to accessing the online group), it was not possible to determine the extent to which accessing the online support group contributed to the self-reported ratings of group efficacy. A final consideration relates to the extent to which respondents actually participate in the online support group. The authors' focus was on exploring the views of those who had accessed the group but did not limit the study to those who had actually posted or replied to a message. Future research may usefully compare active members with those who 'lurk' (i.e., those who read messages but who do not themselves post a message) as evidence suggests (Preece, 2004) that although 'lurkers' do seek answers to questions, their overall satisfaction with the community experience may be lower than those who actively participate.

Section summary

In summary, online support groups may represent a convenient tool to help assist individuals in confronting their debilitating anxiety/phobia and possibly even successfully receive dental care. However, further research needs to be conducted in order to extend these preliminary findings, which would need to take into account the study limitations outlined above and employ a robust **randomised controlled design**. This may be an exciting future avenue for specific phobia research, particularly as this is one of the few treatments that does not involve a therapist, or formal psychological techniques such as graded exposure.

Research investigating treatment in specific phobia: Limitations and future directions

Before we draw the chapter to a close, it is important to consider some of the limitations of studies considering the effectiveness of treatment, and how research in the context of specific phobia should be taken forward. Firstly, it is important to note that there are few long-term follow-up studies of treatment of specific phobia; most follow-ups range from 6 months to a year. Longer-term follow-ups would help us better understand the rates and sources of relapse in specific phobia, and how to improve retention and treatment effects (Choy et al., 2007).

Secondly, studies tend to be of 'completers' – that is individuals who get to the end of the treatment. However, individuals who present for treatment, and complete it, may be particularly motivated and willing to endure anxiety for the end goal and thus may skew the overall picture in terms of effectiveness. Related to this, most studies do not report treatment 'refusal rates' which are known to be high (Garcia-Palacios et al., 2001). In addition, high rate of dropout in studies may affect the interpretation of results; in the studies that Choy et al. reviewed 29 out of 38 reported drop-out rates that varied widely, from zero to 45 per cent. The authors contend that these points highlight that it is likely that many of the treatments covered in this chapter are less effective in the 'real world' when treatment refusal and adherence are taken into account.

Thirdly, Wolitzky-Taylor et al. (2008) note that a significant limitation of almost all the studies in their meta-analysis was the failure to report participants' use of self-guided exposure throughout the period between post-treatment and follow-up. A related limitation, also noted by Choy et al. (2007), is the failure of most studies to report whether their treatment protocol encouraged participants to practice confronting their phobic targets between sessions. They suggest that future studies should report on the level of self-guided exposure after the prescribed treatment protocol is over.

Box 4.6: Treatments in a nutshell

In vivo **treatment**: The most widely used treatment. The patient is presented with the actual fear stimulus.

Virtual reality exposure therapy: The patient is presented with a virtual simulation of the fear stimulus. Used most often for fear of flying and fear of heights.

Systematic/Imaginal therapy: The patient is guided to visualise the fear stimulus.

Cognitive therapy: Patients are guided to realise their fear is irrational; used most often with claustrophobic patients, or those with fear of flying.

Applied muscle tension: Patients are trained to maintain blood pressure during exposure to fear stimulus. For use exclusively with Blood-Injury-Injection phobia.

Medication: Not routinely used with specific phobia patients.

Chapter summary

In this chapter, we have established that individuals with a specific phobia often fail to seek treatment, possibly because they do not want to confront their phobic stimulus. This is unfortunate as there are a number of different psychological treatments available (see Box 4.6 for a brief recap), many of which are based on some form of exposure to the phobic stimulus. Research evidence provides more substantial support for some exposure therapies (i.e., *in vivo* exposure) over others (e.g., systematic desensitization) although there is debate as to whether these differences are maintained in the long term. Newer technologies such as Virtual Reality treatments are continuing to provide strong support in treatment of specific phobia and may be of particular use when the phobic stimulus is logistically difficult to present in a therapist's office (e.g., for flying phobic individuals). Cognitive therapy has been shown to be effective both as a stand-alone therapy and as an adjunct to *in vivo* exposure, but may be most effective for phobias where the individual has anxiety surrounding what will result from the situation. Other treatments which have been more recently proposed (e.g., EMDR, Internet Support Groups), however, still have a small research base. Biological or physiological treatments are rare for specific phobias. Medication is not widely supported, and applied muscle tension is only appropriate for B-I-I phobia patients.

Future research should include long-term follow-ups of participants, report on the number of study completers/refusers and the extent to which participants have exposed themselves to the phobic stimulus between sessions and follow-ups.

⊙ Further reading

Choy, Y., Fyer, A.J., & Lipsitz, J.D. (2007) Treatment of specific phobia in adults. *Clinical Psychology Review*, 27, 266–286.

Coulson, N.S. & Buchanan, H. (2008) Self-reported efficacy of an online dental anxiety support group: A pilot study. *Community Dentistry & Oral Epidemiology*, 36, 43–46.

Grös, D.F. & Antony, M.M. (2006) The assessment and treatment of specific phobias: A review. *Current Psychiatry Reports*, 8, 298–303.

Key search terms

Systematic desensitisation; in vivo exposure, one-session treatment, graded exposure, applied muscle tension.

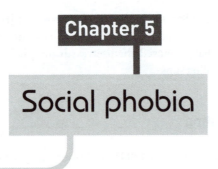

Chapter 5

Social phobia

👁 Introduction

Social phobia is an anxiety disorder which is often characterised by significant and enduring fear which arises through exposure to social or performance situations. The root of the anxiety appears to be the potential for criticism, humiliation or negative evaluation by other individuals. Excessive self-consciousness and self-criticism may lead to extreme phobic avoidance which is the most significant cause of impairment for those with social phobia. Therefore, significant levels of distress or interference in daily functioning are central to the experience of social phobia.

There are two main types of social phobia. Firstly, *Generalised social phobia* relates to a fear of most social interactions together with a fear of most performance situations (e.g. speaking in public or eating in public). Secondly, when an individual is only afraid of one type of performance situation or afraid of only a few rather than most social situations, they are described as having *non-generalised* or *specific social phobia*.

In this chapter, we focus on social phobia and consider its definition and background. We focus on three types of symptoms experienced by sufferers (cognitive, behavioural and physiological). The chapter considers who suffers from social phobia and its relationship with other psychiatric disorders and problem behaviours, such as alcohol misuse. In particular, we focus on the different methods used to diagnose the presence of social phobia and provide some examples of commonly used assessment tools. As there are a number of possible causes of social phobia, we will focus on discussing some of the most commonly cited contributory factors to this condition. Finally, we will consider a number of types of treatments available and discuss how effective they are.

> **In this chapter, we will**
> - Describe social phobia, its symptoms, prevalence and demographic characteristics
> - Discuss the ways in which social phobia is diagnosed
> - Consider a range of possible causes of social phobia
> - Discuss different types of treatments and how effective they are

Historical background

Whilst the first literary description of social anxiety and shyness can be traced back to Hippocrates 400 BC (Heckelman & Schneier, 1995), the earliest explicit references to social phobia were made in the early 1900s by Janet (1903) who described 'phobie des situations sociales'. Later, in the 1930s the term 'social neurosis' was used by Schilder (1938) to describe extremely shy patients. In the 1950s interest grew significantly in behavioural therapy for phobias and it was the British psychiatrist Isaac Marks who proposed that social phobias could be regarded as a distinct category (Marks, 1969; Marks & Gelder, 1966). Over time this concept was gradually acknowledged by the APA and in 1980 social phobia was included as a psychiatric diagnosis by APA (1980) in the third edition of the Diagnostic and Statistical Manual of Mental Disorders (DSM-III).

After the inclusion of social phobia in DSM-III, there was little attention given by researchers to the disorder and it was indeed referred to as 'the neglected anxiety disorder' (Leibowitz et al., 1985) and this persisted until the middle of the 1980s. Since then, however, there has been a significant rise in the number of research studies that have examined this disorder.

◉ What is social phobia?

According to the Diagnostic and Statistical Manual of Mental Disorders (DSM-IV-TR) (see Chapter 1 for details) social phobia (also known as social anxiety disorder) is 'a marked and persistent fear of one or more social or performance situations in which the person is exposed to unfamiliar people or to possible scrutiny by others. The individual fears that he or she will act in a way (or show anxiety symptoms) that will be humiliating or embarrassing' (APA, 2000, p. 456).

At the core of social phobia is a significant fear of being observed or scrutinised by people who are unfamiliar to the individual. More specifically, the sufferer may find it extremely distressing when they think that they may perform inadequately or show signs of nervousness which may result in embarrassment or humiliation. The individual who suffers from social phobia may find that their fears are restricted to specific contexts or settings, such as formal public appearances (e.g., making a speech at a wedding) or they may experience their fears across a range of different situations such as eating or writing in public, using public toilets, attending social gatherings or dealing with authorities and so on.

When an individual encounters phobic situations, or anticipates that they may encounter a phobic situation, they may experience a range of anxiety symptoms including: sweating, palpitations, blushing or **catastrophic thinking**. These symptoms may manifest themselves and continue even when the individual realises that their reaction is exaggerated and unreasonable. As a result, the individual may continue to avoid such social situations or if they do encounter the situation then it is endured under significant anxiety.

The symptoms may have a profound impact on their daily lives and routines, relationships, social activities and work-related performance (Stein & Kean, 2000). In cases where the social phobic is under 18, the DSM-IV criteria require that the symptoms have been experienced for a minimum duration of 6 months. In addition, other possible medical ailments or conditions or other anxiety disorders should not better account for the symptoms experienced.

What are the symptoms of social phobia?

Broadly speaking, there are three main categories of symptoms linked to social phobia: cognitive, behavioural and physiological. An individual living with social phobia may experience any combination of these symptoms. Let's take a look at each of these in turn (see Box 5.1 for example).

Cognitive symptoms

Individuals with social phobia are typically very concerned with how they feel they are being perceived and evaluated by others around them (see Box 5.1). This social anxiety may result from an excess of negative thoughts, perceived personal shortcomings, excessively high standards for one's own behaviour/performance and/or unrealistic beliefs about the standards people use to evaluate others. The symptoms which typically are associated with social phobia may manifest themselves prior to, during or after leaving a particular setting or context (Wells & Clark, 1997).

Behavioural symptoms

Social phobia is more than normal shyness! Rather, it is a persistent fear that one or more situations which the individual encounters might lead to scrutiny by others. The social phobic fears that they may say or do something that might embarrass or humiliate them in such a situation. As such, it may lead to social avoidance and significant social or occupational/educational difficulties. For example, a promising employee might decline the opportunity for promotion in fear that it would lead to greater social interactions. Alternatively, a student may remain quiet and disengaged in class because they may be too frightened to speak up publicly (see Box 5.1, the example of Amy who missed her first University class). According to the principles of **operant conditioning** (Skinner, 1974), phobias are thought to be maintained through escape and avoidance behaviours. Indeed, whilst these avoidance behaviours may well reduce the anxiety experienced in the short-term, they do not in fact help the individual learn more appropriate ways to deal with the feared situation or setting. According to Wells & Clark (1997), social phobics are likely to engage in what they describe as 'safety behaviours' such as using alcohol or avoiding eye contact (see Box 5.1, the example of David).

Physiological symptoms

The physiological symptoms experienced in social phobia such as palpitations, sweating, shakes or hot flushes either during or in anticipation of exposure (see Box 5.1, the example of David) to the feared situation are similar to those experienced in other anxiety-related disorders (Rapee, 1995). These symptoms of **arousal** originate from over-activity of the sympathetic division of the **autonomic nervous system** and are typical features of the **'fight or flight'** response (Cannon, 1927). This arousal is also associated with raised blood pressure and secretion of stress hormones initiated by the **hypothalamus–pituitary gland–adrenocortical axis**.

Box 5.1: Some examples of people living with social phobia

Amy is 20 years old and a first-year student doing a degree in sociology. During the induction week Amy was too scared to attend as she knew that it was common for the academic teacher to invite all students to introduce themselves and say a little about where they have come from and what they like doing. The thought of this was too much for Amy and she was convinced that she'd stutter or make a fool of herself if she spoke to the class. Amy decided to miss her first day so she could avoid speaking publicly in class.

David is 16 years old and has recently found it more difficult to interact with others at school. He avoids public areas in lunch breaks because he feels everyone is laughing at him and making fun of the way he talks. As he walks along the school corridors he keeps his eyes firmly to the ground so that he doesn't have to make eye contact with anyone. His heart races until he gets home from school but even then he starts to dread going back the next day.

Mark is 36 and an administrator; as part of his job he sometimes has to ring clients. He is absolutely petrified of speaking to clients on the phone because he feels he always messes it up. He is convinced that they will be too busy to speak to him or he will give the wrong information to them and they will be annoyed at his incompetence. Once the call is made, Mark is convinced that it didn't go well as he replays in his mind what was said and the more he does this the more he believes that the phone call didn't go well.

Sue is 53 and is dreading the fact that she has to attend a staff meeting soon and is likely to be asked to make a short presentation to the team. Although it is a few days away she has already found it difficult to sleep as she worries about how she will perform. In her mind she can see herself getting mixed up or forgetting what she has to say and is scared she will faint. She describes the anticipation as awful!

How common is social phobia?

As a result of changes in the diagnostic criteria and the differences in how social phobia has been measured, estimates have varied considerably, but when using the latest most up-to-date diagnostic criteria, estimates range from approximately 4 to 14 per cent of the adult population (Ansseau et al., 1999; Kringlen et al., 2001).

Social phobia is most likely to begin during early to mid-adolescence (Faravelli et al., 2000; Mannuzza et al., 1990), though some studies have found it to be present in younger children (Beidel et al., 2000). It is usually the case that as children get older they begin to become concerned about what other people might think of them. As a result, the awareness of potentially being negatively judged by others begins around the age of 8 years. Therefore, the appearance of social phobia in younger children is likely to be rare. Onset of social phobia after the age of 25 appears to be rare (Wittchen et al., 1999a), but not impossible. Furthermore, we generally regard social phobia as a chronic condition, indeed it is not uncommon for individuals with the disorder to have had it for 10 years or more (Davidson et al., 1993; Perugi et al., 1990).

Gender differences and socio-demographic patterns

In most studies of the general adult population social phobia appears to be more common in females as compared to males (ratio of three to two). However, in **clinical populations** the ratio is approximately equal or males are reported to be slightly in the majority (Heimberg & Juster, 1995). This suggests that perhaps males are more likely to seek treatment for their social phobia, potentially because the consequences of it are seen as more serious in the context of their everyday lives.

Social phobia has also been shown to be more common in those from a poorer background, lower social class, single or unmarried, unemployed or have a poor educational background (Degonda & Angst, 1993; Wittchen et al., 1999a). However, it is difficult to establish whether these are the causes or consequences of social phobia and further research is required to determine the direction of causality.

Co-morbidity

It appears to be the case that social phobia is more often than not associated with other psychiatric disorders. Indeed, **lifetime comorbidity** has been reported to range from 69 per cent (Schneier et al., 1992) to 92 per cent (Faravelli et al., 2000). One study, for example, conducted in the adult population of Germany found that only 12 per cent of all cases diagnosed as social phobia were 'pure' (Jacobi et al., 2002). That is to say, all other cases had at least one other type of psychiatric disorder present. In particular, depression as well as other anxiety disorders and substance abuse appear to be associated with social phobia (Magee et al., 1996).

If we have a look at the timeline involved, in the majority of cases the social phobia begins before the onset of major depression (De Graaf et al., 2003; Weiller et al., 1996). Moreover, it is also associated with a more troublesome course of an already existing depression, such as shorter intervals between episodes or more depressive symptoms.

Social phobia is also linked with alcohol misuse, for example, Randall et al. (2001a) reported that approximately 20 per cent of patients being treated for social phobia and 15 per cent of people who were receiving treatment for alcohol misuse (see Box 5.2) had both disorders. However, it is fair to say that there has been a lack of well designed and controlled studies that have explored the relationship between the two.

Box 5.2: Alcohol use in social phobia: A complicated partnership?

A number of studies have reported that individuals may use alcohol as a means of coping with social fears as well as stress. According to the 'tension reduction hypothesis' – alcohol may serve as a negative reinforcer (something that stops an unpleasant experience). It is thought that when an individual feels less anxious or stressed after drinking alcohol, they are more likely to consume alcohol in the future for its stress/anxiety-reducing qualities. A contentious issue is whether alcohol actually reduces stress (Carrigan & Randall, 2003). Indeed, according to a number of researchers, if the pharmacological qualities of alcohol are considered, it should actually lead to an increase in stress and that as a result negative reinforcement using alcohol would be ineffective (Spencer & Hutchinson, 1999).

If asked, an individual with social phobia is likely to report that consuming alcohol is a common technique used to help cope with the disorder. Why is this so? It appears to be the case that the beliefs or expectancies an individual has about the anxiety-reducing qualities of alcohol play an important role in this relationship. Indeed, there has been a number of research studies conducted which have explored the role of alcohol beliefs or expectancies and these have shown that both positive and negative expectations about alcohol can be important (see Carrigan & Randall, 2003 for a review of the literature). In fact, it may well be the case that these expectancies (and differences in them) account for the fact that not everyone with social phobia drinks alcohol to cope with their social fears. For example, people who think that alcohol might make things worse may be less likely to drink it as it may increase their fears about looking stupid in front of others.

A positive expectancy that alcohol can help reduce social fears may explain why some individuals choose to use it as a means of coping. However, if this positive expectancy is not addressed then it may be an influential factor in why an individual continues to drink alcohol to deal with anxiety. On the other hand, a subset of social phobics may in fact experience a genuine pharmacological effect and reduction in social fears. Whilst they may have started drinking alcohol as a coping strategy, they may continue to do so because they experience symptom reduction when they do. However, there have been few good-quality research studies which have explored the expectancies surrounding alcohol and it's chances of reducing social fears, and how expectancies are in fact related to drinking alcohol or have shown reliably that drinking alcohol leads to a reduction in social fears (Carrigan & Randall, 2003). It seems that the majority of studies have used student samples who do not have any formal diagnosis of social phobia, rather than clinical samples of individuals who have a formal diagnosis. Regardless of the fact that researchers have not been able to ascertain definitively whether drinking alcohol actually helps social phobics by reducing social fears, there are many individuals with social phobia who believe that it does and use it to cope with their anxiety. Going forward, some of these individuals are likely to develop alcohol-related problems on top of their existing social phobia. As a result, there is an increased risk to these individuals, for example, accidents as well as interpersonal conflicts and relationship difficulties.

How do we diagnose social phobia?

The diagnosis of social phobia is typically made on the basis of the patient's history and the symptoms that have been experienced. It may also be the case that the doctor or health professional screens the individual for other disorders in order to rule them out, for example, other anxiety-related disorders, depression or phobias. The diagnosis of social phobia plays an important role in describing an individual's impairment, influencing the intervention technique and guiding the on going treatment decisions and process.

Diagnosing social phobia in children

When attempting to diagnose a child, the doctor or health professional must acknowledge that children don't experience the same freedom as adults do when it comes to avoiding social situations that scare them.

Therefore, they may not be able to fully explain what it is about the situation that frightens them. It is also important to evaluate the ability of the child to develop social relationships with people that they know and to assess their interactions with peers for signs of social phobia. There are a number of diagnostic tools which can be used and this includes child versions of tools used for the diagnosis of social phobia in adults.

Assessment tools

There are a range of recommended but distinct methods that can be used for the assessment of social phobia that are similar to the methods used to diagnose and assess specific phobias (see Chapter 2). These include: diagnostic interview, clinician-administered scales, self-report scales and behavioural assessment. Let's have a look at each of these.

Diagnostic interview

A diagnostic (or clinical) interview is simply an interaction between professional and patient in which a series of questions are asked in order to determine whether the patient meets the criteria for a certain illness. These interviews can be structured or have some flexibility (as in semi-structured) and use different sources of information to reach a conclusion. There are a number of advantages to using semi-structured clinical interviews in that they use patient report, **behavioural observation** as well as a clinician's own judgement to come to a comprehensive and thorough diagnostic assessment. These interviews are also helpful with the evaluation of **co-morbid** conditions, an issue important in the assessment of social phobia since fear of social evaluation often co-occurs with features such as **agoraphobic avoidance**, panic attacks, social withdrawal, rumination and dysthymia (a chronic mood disorder).

Examples of Semi-Structured Clinical Interviews (which can be used for social phobia)

- *Anxiety Disorders Interview Schedule for DSM-IV (ADIS-IV)*
  This is a frequently used diagnostic interview that assesses major anxiety disorders, substance use disorders, mood disorders and disorders that frequently overlap with anxiety disorders, for example, hypochondriasis. A useful feature of this diagnostic interview is a Clinician Severity Rating (CSR) scale, which allows the clinician to record a severity rating for each diagnosis ranging from zero (absent) to eight (very severely disabling).

- *Structured Clinical Interview for DSM-IV Axis 1 Disorders (SCID-I/P)*
  This is a semi-structured clinical interview that can be administered by a clinician or trained mental health professional. Although it is a lengthy interview and requires extensive training, it is flexible and can be used for research purposes and also includes an overview section to obtain **socio-occupational** and other background details.

Clinician-administered scales

The two most commonly used instruments for social phobia are described below. Clinician-rated psychometric instruments offer the brevity of an itemised scale as well as the flexibility of clinical judgement coupled with behavioural observation.

Examples of Clinician-Administered Scales

- *Leibowitz Social Anxiety Scale (LSAS) (Leibowitz, 1987)*
  This is the most widely used clinician-administered scale for social phobia assessment. It was designed to cover the full range of the two facets of social phobia (i.e., performance situations and social interaction) that individuals with social phobia fear and avoid. This is a 24-item scale with 13 situations that are performance-related (e.g., 'participating in a small group') and 11 situations that are social interactions (e.g., 'going to a party'). The clinician describes each situation to the individual who in turn rates the intensity of anxiety experienced when faced with that situation ranging from zero (none) to three (severe) and the frequency of their avoidance of the situation ranging from zero (never) to three (usually). Four sub-scores are created from this (Performance Fear, Performance Avoidance, Social Fear, and Social Avoidance). An overall score can also be created by summing fear and avoidance ratings across all situations.
- *Brief Social Phobia Scale (BSPS) (Davidson et al., 1997)*
  This scale is a symptom-rating scale that was developed in order to assess social phobia severity and symptom change over time with treatment. The scale contains 11 checklist items, seven that describe specific phobia situations that the individual must rate on a severity scale of fear ranging from zero (none) to four (extreme) and a frequency scale of avoidance ranging from zero (never) to four

(always). There are four additional items that reflect physiological symptoms associated with encountering or anticipating feared situations (e.g., blushing) that the individual must rate using the aforementioned severity-rating scale. This scale yields three sub-scores (Fear, Avoidance and Physiology) as well as an overall score ranging from 0 to 72, with a score of 20 or above the cut-off for generalised social phobia.

Self-report scales

Arguably, the most time-efficient assessment tools are self-report scales. They are helpful when repeated evaluation is required and are useful in treatment studies that are being conducted in several locations and require frequent symptom monitoring. In recent times there has been a growing use of self-report scales for social phobia in research studies.

Examples of self-report scales

- *Social Phobia and Anxiety Inventory (SPAI) (Turner et al., 1989)*
  The SPAI was developed to assess social anxiety distress across a range of **somatic symptoms**, cognitions and behaviour across fear-producing situations. The scale includes a set of 45 items reflecting social-situation anxiety, somatic symptoms and phobic conditions. Thirteen items assess **agoraphobia** symptoms. Each of the situational items includes separate ratings of distress for interactions with four groups of people: (1) strangers, (2) figures of authority, (3) the opposite sex and (4) people in general. For the two cognitive items, individuals are asked to rate five types of anticipatory thoughts (e.g., 'I will probably make a mistake and look foolish') and four types of **in vivo** thoughts (e.g. 'I wish I could leave and avoid the whole situation'). Similarly, each of the somatic items needs a separate rating for the physiological symptom experienced in the situation: (1) sweating, (2) blushing and (3) shaking. Therefore, most of the items in this scale have sub-components and this means that an individual has 109 individual ratings to make, ranging from one (Never) to seven (Always). The social phobia sub-scale score ranges from 0 to 192, with 60 being used as a cut-off for social phobia. For the agoraphobia scale, scores range from 0 to 78. The SPAI difference score is done by subtracting the agoraphobia score from the social phobia sub-scale score.

Therefore, the SPAI offers the chance to remove avoidance behaviour due to agoraphobia rather than social phobia.

- *The Social Phobia Scale and the Social Interaction Anxiety Scale (SPS and SIAS) (Mattick & Clarke, 1998)*

  The SPS and SIAS were originally developed as separate self-report measures of social anxiety; however, they are often administered together. The SPS reflects fears of scrutiny during observation by others, whereas the SIAS assesses anxiety experienced during interaction with other people. The SPS has 20 items that individuals must rate with regard to how characteristic or true they are for them on a scale ranging from zero (Not at all) to four (Extremely). Items include both worries about signs of nervousness (e.g., 'I fear I may blush when I am with others') as well as scrutiny of performance (e.g., 'I become anxious if I have to write in front of others'). The SIAS also has 20 items which reflect discomfort in social settings (e.g., 'I am tense mixing in a group') and include **dyadic** interactions (e.g., 'I tense up if I meet an acquaintance on the street'). Scores can range from zero to eight for each scale with a suggested cut-off score of 34 for the SIAS (i.e., generalised social phobia) and 24 for the SPS (i.e., non-generalised social phobia).

- *The Social Phobia Inventory (SPIN) (Connor et al., 2000)*

  A more recently developed scale is the Social Phobia Inventory (SPIN) which was developed in order to assess the full range of symptoms associated with social phobia, including fear, avoidance, as well as physiological symptoms. The SPIN has 17 items that individuals must rate on a five-point scale ranging from zero (Not at all) to four (Extremely). Items include 'I avoid talking to people I don't know', 'Sweating in front of people causes me distress' and 'Being embarrassed or looking stupid are among my worst fears'. The scale has shown that it can used as a screening tool and also as a means of determining whether there is any improvement in symptoms as a result of treatment.

What causes social phobia?

Much has been written about the possible causes of social phobia from many different perspectives. As yet, there is no clear definitive answer to this question. Researchers from a variety of backgrounds have considered this question and we shall now look at some of the possible reasons. In particular, we shall consider the following two broad types of explanation:

Psychological/environmental explanations

- past experience
- cultural influences
- social factors
- family factors

Biological explanations

- genetic factors
- neural mechanisms

We will finish this section by considering psychological explanations for the maintenance of social phobia and, in particular, the 'cognitive model' of social phobia developed by Clark & Wells (1995). This model has proven to be very popular explanation as to why social phobia can be a persistent problem and has influenced current patterns of psychological treatment.

Psychological/environmental explanations

Past experience

According to **classical conditioning** models (see Chapter 3 for a brief overview), the origins of social phobia may rest in bad or traumatic experiences in the past. A social situation may potentially become feared through its learned association with past negative experiences (Mineka & Zinbarg, 1995). For example, whilst at school a pupil might be asked to stand up and talk to the class (becoming the conditioned stimuli). This might result in the pupil being made fun of and laughed at (the unconditioned stimuli); therefore this social situation may create feelings of anxiety or fear in the future (a conditioned response). Indeed, there is some evidence for such: those who suffer from social phobia, when asked, suggest that it arose in such conditioning experiences (Stemberger et al., 1995). This type of explanation seems to be more commonly associated with performance-related social phobia, for example, public speaking. However, it is not just direct experiences which can be important but also seeing or hearing about bad social experiences of others (known as 'vicarious or observational learning'). Social phobia may also be linked to the long-term effects of being ignored, bullied and rejected or simply 'not fitting in'. In a number of studies, childhood experiences of peer rejection and social isolation have been described by social phobics (e.g. Rapee & Melville, 1997).

Cultural influences

Cultural factors have also been shown to be related to social phobia partly through the reaction of society to shyness, avoidance and shame. For example, in the context of parenting, some studies have found that American children were more likely to develop social phobia if their parents use shame as a disciplinary technique and they emphasise the importance of others' opinions. However, this association was not present for Chinese/Chinese-American children (Leung et al., 1994). Indeed, in China, research has shown that shy and inhibited children are more accepted than non-shy or less-inhibited peers and more likely to be seen as competent (Xinyin et al., 1995).

Social factors

It has also been suggested that difficulties in developing social skills (i.e., skills related to communication or interaction with others) may be related to social phobia. This could be through an inability or lack of confidence to interact in social situations and elicit positive reactions and acceptance from other individuals. Research on these specific aspects has been mixed, with some studies reporting problems with social skills and others not reporting this problem. However, it does appear to be the case that individuals who are socially anxious do consider their own social skills to be lacking (Segrin & Kinney, 2005).

Whilst the findings relating to the role of social skills deficits in adults has been mixed, there appears to be more convincing evidence for the role of social skills deficits in children with social phobia. Spence et al. (1999) reported that compared with non-anxious children, social phobic children did show relatively poorer social skills and social competence as assessed by parent and child reports and actual behavioural observation both at school and during role play tasks.

Spence et al. (1999) has argued that social skill deficits will lead to a lack of success in social situations and in turn this may result in an expectation of poor outcomes and negative thoughts relating to future situations in which evaluation and scrutiny by others is likely. These negative thoughts and expectations may then generate emotional and physiological responses such as anxiety and avoidance behaviour. Furthermore, this anxiety is thought to limit the effective use of social skills, therefore leading to poorer social performance. The avoidance of social situations was also suggested to reduce the chances to learn about social skills and further perpetuating the social anxiety cycle. According to this thinking, a child could develop social phobia if they experience any difficulties at any point in the cycle. What is important to note is that this explanation for social phobia does not rule out the contribution of any other type of explanation (e.g., genetic, family influences and so on) but it does suggest that treatment needs to include a combination of social skills training, increased social opportunities, **cognitive restructuring** and anxiety reduction techniques in order to address each part of the anxiety cycle.

Family factors

Social phobia has also been linked to the interactions which take place between parents and their children. For example, a number of studies have shown that the children of parents who suffer from major depression are at an increased risk of developing social phobia. Indeed, if parents themselves are socially anxious then a child also might develop social fears and avoidance behaviours through a **modelling** process (Bandura, 1977). Children of socially anxious or depressed parents may encounter fewer social situations as they grow up, perhaps because their parents are less inclined to socialise with others. This would mean that a socially anxious child would have fewer opportunities to develop key social skills that could help them deal successfully with social situations. Moreover, social phobics have often described their parents as being overprotective and such a parenting style might contribute to fearful or socially withdrawn behaviour in children (Hudson & Rapee, 2000).

Why does social phobia persist?

As we saw in Chapters 2–4, for many individuals with a specific phobia, it can be relatively easy to avoid the object (e.g., a snake) that causes the phobic reaction or situation. It is thought that this avoidance is one reason as to why the phobia may persist, but the same cannot be said for social phobia. For individuals living with social phobia, it is unlikely that they will be able to avoid the feared situations and, therefore, the question becomes: If social phobics don't avoid these situations, but in fact encounter them fairly often, why then does their phobia persist? In order to provide a possible explanation for this, the cognitive model of social phobia has been proposed (Clark & Wells, 1995; Wells & Clark, 1997).

A psychological explanation for the maintenance of social phobia: The cognitive model

According to this model, when a social phobic enters a social situation a number of assumptions are activated. There are three types of assumptions, according to this model:

(1) *Excessively high standards for social performance*
Examples: '*I must always appear confident and intelligent*' or '*I must be witty and fun*'.

(2) *Conditional beliefs concerning the consequences of performing in a certain way*
Examples: '*If people get to know me, they will not like me*' or '*If I am quiet, people will think I'm not very interesting*'.

(3) *Unconditional negative beliefs about the individual*
Examples: '*I'm not very interesting*' or '*I'm weird*' or '*I'm not very bright*'.

As a consequence of these assumptions, social phobics may think a social situation is dangerous and that they will somehow not perform as well as they feel they should do and that often ambiguous social cues are a sign that others around them are judging them negatively. If the social phobic thinks of a situation in this way they will then become anxious. It then becomes something of a vicious cycle as the phobic begins to monitor and observe themselves. They then use this internal information to infer how others are evaluating them but are unable to accept (or ignore) any information, or responses from others, which appears to argue against how they see themselves.

The internal information which is used by the social phobic can be grouped broadly into three categories. Firstly, if a social phobic feels anxious they believe that they look anxious (i.e., they think that others around them will be able to spot signs of anxiety, such as a red face or sweating). Second, they may experience images of themselves as if from the perspective of those around them. However, these images are not in fact what others would see, but rather are visualisations of their fears. Third, the individual might *feel* different and apart from others around them.

Another important factor which may contribute to the maintenance of the social phobia is that of 'safety behaviours'. These are actions undertaken by the individual in feared situations that are intended to prevent a feared **catastrophic event**. For example, these behaviours may include: avoiding eye contact, using alcohol, holding a glass tightly, a reluctance to disclose personal information and so on. However, if the catastrophe that is feared by the social phobic doesn't happen (e.g., if a social phobic fears that people around them will laugh at them and if people do not laugh), then the phobic believes that this was as a result of engaging in the safety behaviours rather than due to the situation being less dangerous than they previously thought.

There are different types of safety behaviours that a social phobic can engage in. Indeed, some of these behaviours are actually mental processes. For example, a phobic who is scared of speaking to someone in case they don't make sense might memorise what they wish to say and compare it with what they are saying as the conversation unfolds. Sometimes the safety behaviours can actually make their symptoms worse. For example, someone might keep their arms close to them to stop others seeing them sweat and this might actually make the sweating worse.

Also, for many safety behaviours, engaging in them actually leads the individual to be more self aware and the level of self-focussed attention and monitoring increases and this may actually serve to enhance the individual's negative self-image. Safety behaviours can also draw attention more to the individual. For example, someone who speaks very quietly and slowly may find that others around them focus on the individual even more. Finally, sometimes the safety behaviours actually influence others around them and this leads to the phobic's fears actually being realised. For example, in an effort to hide the fact they are anxious, social phobics may sometimes come across as distant or aloof. Others around them might therefore think that the social phobic does not like them and so interact with them in a less positive or warm way.

The cognitive model places a particular focus on self-focused attention and the role of internal information to create a distorted impression of how one might be seen in a social situation. It has been argued by Clark & Wells (1995) that social phobia is in part maintained by a reduced level of processing of external social cues. Furthermore, they suggest that this reduced level of processing of external social cues is actually biased in a negative way. For example, the social phobic is more likely to recall signs from others around them that suggest that they are being negatively judged. However, the reality is perhaps that the social phobic is picking up on very ambiguous cues and interpreting them (incorrectly) as signs of disapproval and so on.

For many social phobics, there is considerable anxiety just thinking about a forthcoming social interaction. They may think through what they believe might happen and in so doing this may create feelings of anxiety and they begin to dwell on past examples where things have gone wrong for them. Sometimes the anxiety may be too much and they avoid the situation altogether; however, if they do engage in the social situation then they are already focused on the self and are monitoring themselves closely. If there are signs by others that everything is okay and they are being accepted, then the social phobic may be more likely to miss or ignore these cues because they are so self-focussed.

When the social phobic is able to exit the social situation that is not sadly an end to their anxiety and distress, however, their levels of anxiety are likely to have declined as there is no longer an immediate threat. Furthermore, they are unlikely to have obtained from the social situation a clear and unambiguous sign from others that the interaction went well and others approve of them. As a consequence, the social phobic may engage in a post mortem of the event (Clark & Wells, 1995) (see the case of Mark as an illustration – Box 5.1). That is to say, they will review every aspect of the social interaction and tend to focus on their own negative view of their performance and often will conclude that the interaction was far more negative than they first thought. The social phobic is also likely to recall past experiences and (incorrect) examples of poor performance in the social situation and this most current example is added to the list of failures in social situations. The consequence is that the phobic has now gathered even more (incorrect) evidence of their failings and poor performance in social situations.

Biological explanations

Genetic factors

There is a growing body of research that has examined the genetic basis of social phobia and it would appear that genetic factors do indeed play a significant though modest role in the development of social phobia. If we look back at some of the earliest studies into this issue (e.g., Bruch & Heimberg, 1994) we find that higher rates of social phobia were found among close family members of people with social phobia (e.g., parents, offspring, siblings). For example, children with social phobia were more likely to have parents with social phobia compared to their peers. Furthermore, children of parents with social phobia were found to be at increased risk from this condition (Lieb et al., 2000; Mancini et al., 1996).

We are now in a position where there are a number of large-scale twin studies that have found there to be a significant but modest genetic role in the development of social phobia (e.g. Kendler et al., 1999). Indeed, more recently, Beatty et al. (2002) undertook a **meta-analysis** and reported an estimate of heritability of 0.65; however, other researchers have suggested a somewhat lower estimate ranging from 0.4 to 0.5 (Ollendick & Hirshfeld Becker, 2002).

Neural mechanisms

Whilst the exact neural bases for social phobia are not clear, there has been a growing amount of research that has examined the role of specific neurochemicals, as well as functioning of specific parts of the brain. It is known that sociability is associated with **dopamine** neurotransmission; indeed, use of stimulants such as amphetamines to increase self-confidence and improve social abilities is commonplace. Also, social phobia has been linked to an imbalance in **serotonin** (Brunello et al., 2000). Serotonin is involved in modulating mood, emotions, sleep and appetite and is involved in the transmission of impulses between nerve cells. It is thought that individuals with social phobia may have receptors that are extra-sensitive to serotonin, which then leads to fluctuations in nerve impulses (Tancer, 1993). As part of the limbic system, the **amygdala** is related to fear cognition and emotional learning (Adolphs et al., 1997; Bechara et al., 1995). It has been reported that individuals who suffer from social phobia may have a hyper-sensitive amygdale. Other research suggests a role for the **anterior cingulated cortex**, which is known to be involved in how people experience physical pain. It would appear that this area may also be involved in the experience of 'social pain', such as perceiving group exclusion (Eisenberger et al., 2003).

Social phobia: Could it be the result of 'a bit of everything'?

Given the many potential causes of social phobia, it is unlikely that one single factor is accountable for the development of this disorder. Rather, it is likely to be a complex interplay between genetic and environmental factors. Even though past experiences which may have been traumatic or distressing can be potentially significant, it is also possible that socially anxious individuals learn fear reactions more easily than do non-anxious

individuals as a result of genetic factors. Together, this inherited vulnerability and exposure to environmental stressors may lead to the acquisition
of the social fear. Thus, social phobia may well be maintained as a result
of sufferers engaging in avoidance behaviours and cognitive biases.

Section summary

In this section we have considered the nature of social phobia, its symptoms and prevalence as well as some of the main ways in which it can be
diagnosed. As we have seen, there are a number of possible explanations
for the development of social phobia, all with some evidence. Moreover,
we have learnt how social phobia may persist and how the cognitive model
has been influential in understanding social phobia. Next, we turn our
attention to the treatment of social phobia.

◉ Treatment of social phobia

In the 1990s we witnessed a significant rise in the number of research
studies examining social phobia. As a consequence, there was also an
increase in the number of studies which examined treatments for social
phobia. Generally speaking, there are two broad categories of treatment:
psychological treatment and biological treatments (i.e., drug treatment).

Psychological treatments

Cognitive Behavioural Therapy (CBT)

Cognitive behavioural therapy is a talking therapy that aims to solve the
problems faced by an individual through a goal-oriented, systematic procedure. Cognitive behavioural group therapy following the principles of
Heimberg & Barlow (1988) was one of the first to be assessed in terms of
its effectiveness (see Heimberg & Juster (1995) for a review of the literature). This approach included **simulated exposure** to feared situations,
cognitive restructuring, and homework tasks for *in vivo* **exposure**. Typically, this group therapy operates with between six and eight individuals
and two therapists and lasts for normally 12 weeks with three hours per
week. Of the studies that have examined this type of treatment, the evidence suggests that it is beneficial, even up to 5 years after the treatment
programme had been completed (Heimberg et al., 1993b).

Using their cognitive model of social phobia (see Cognitive Model earlier in this chapter), Clark & Wells (1995) have developed an influential

cognitive behavioural therapy treatment programme which does share a number of similarities with Heimberg's group therapy, but places more focus on the identification and modification of safety behaviours and the use of the correction of distorted self-processing. Cognitive behavioural therapy which is based on this model has been shown to be particularly effective (Clark et al., 2006).

The key steps in CBT based on the cognitive model of social phobia

As we have seen, the model proposed by Clark & Wells focusses on the role of self-focused attention, **negative self-processing** and safety behaviours. As a result, the therapy emphasises the need to address these features and help social phobics to process information more positively and in a way which will help them recognise disconfirming negative beliefs by direct observation of the social situation, rather than oneself.

It is often challenging when trying to work with social phobics since the therapy is in itself a social interaction, something that we know social phobics can dread. The social phobic may indeed display a number of the safety behaviours we have outlined earlier in this chapter and they may present themselves as aloof or uninterested. It is important that the therapist is aware of this and as the therapy continues, and improvements are made, the phobic may indeed become more relaxed and the social interaction, much easier to deal with.

(1) *Deriving a patient-specific version of the model*
The first task in the process is to tease out a patient-specific overview of their social phobia. This is done by asking the patient to relate an episode or example in which they became anxious. The therapist will ask questions to explore their fears, for example:

- What went through your mind in that, or anticipation of that, situation?
- What did you think was the worst that could happen? Was there anything that you thought people might notice?
- If they did notice, what do you think they would think?
- What would that mean to you?

As the therapist explores their social fears, the aim is to try and get to that 'bottom line', that is, the worst thing that could happen, the feared catastrophic event.

It is also important to identify all the safety behaviours that an individual might engage in. As we have noted previously, safety behaviours may prevent an individual from realising that their worst fears may not have come true. The therapist will ask the individual to describe what they did to prevent their social fear from happening, prevent it from being noticed by others or prevent them from being negatively judged by others. This is repeated for each social fear that the individual has identified.

(2) *Manipulation of self-focussed attention and safety behaviours*
In social situations, social phobics are preoccupied with themselves, and hence their attention is largely taken up by monitoring their symptoms of anxiety and undertaking safety behaviours. This means that there is little attention actually being paid to what is going on in the social situation. In order to begin to address this, the individual is asked to role play a feared situation. They are asked to do this twice, the first time using safety behaviours and focusing on themselves, and the second time trying not to engage in any safety behaviours and focus on what is actually going on in the social situation. After each role play the individual is asked to rate how anxious they were, how anxious they felt they appeared and how well they thought they had performed. It is also common for these role plays to be video taped. The purpose of this task is to show to the patient that when they don't engage in safety behaviours and are not self-focussed, they actually feel less anxious and perform better. This is an important first step in addressing social phobia and is often supported by tasks which the individual can do at home and which ask them to focus externally (i.e., to focus on what is going on outwith themselves) and not use safety behaviours in social situations.

(3) *Video feedback*
The next step is to help individuals get more objective and realistic information about how they actually perform in social situations. One means through which this can be achieved is through video feedback. Indeed, video feedback may be used several times during the CBT sessions. Before watching the video feedback, the individual is asked to think about the role plays and picture how they came across. They are asked to indicate all the ways in which their fears will be revealed and how they will show up on the video feedback. The individual is instructed to view the video as if they were watching a stranger and not to focus on how they were feeling at the time. Once they have seen the video the individual compares how they actually came across with how they thought they

would come across. Typically, this activity helps the individual realise that they did not in fact come across as badly as they thought they had. For example, an individual might fear that their hand would shake uncontrollably when speaking but on watching the feedback learn that it was hardly noticeable, if at all.

(4) *Shift of attention and interrogation of the social environment*
The next step in the therapy is to work with individuals to shift their attention from an internal focus to an external one and to avoid using safety behaviours during therapeutic sessions as well as home-based tasks. Similar to other types of cognitive behavioural programmes, the individual is asked to confront their feared situations. However, what is different is the way in which the exposure to the situation is used. Rather than simply being exposed repeatedly to the feared situation, the exposure is used by the individual to test out predictions about the fears the individual has about the situation. In order to test out negative predictions, the behavioural experiment and survey method have proven to be popular.

Behavioural experiment

In a behavioural experiment, the individual is asked to enter an anxiety-laden social situation in order to find out whether their social fears occur. In the behavioural experiment, their social fears are examined in order. Firstly, do the feared symptoms occur as frequently or severely as they believed they would? Secondly, when the feared symptoms do occur, are they as visible as the individual thinks they are? Thirdly, when the feared symptoms occur and are visible, are the symptoms noticed by others as much as the individual believes they will be? Finally, when the feared symptoms occur and are visible and are noticed by others, is the phobic judged as negatively as they think they will be? It is very important that the social phobic actively tests out each of these four questions or else their **catastrophic beliefs** about what might happen if someone did notice their feared symptom might persist. The term 'widening the bandwith' was coined by Clark and Wells for this exercise as it helps individuals discover that there is a range of ways in which it is acceptable to behave in social situations. Getting the individual to specify in advance how others would react to the unacceptable behaviour is an important feature of this step.

As the cognitive behavioural therapy moves on, it is important that the phobic is able to set up and undertake these behavioural experiments for homework, reviewing the outcome and creating further experiments with the therapist in the treatment sessions. As the number of behavioural experiments increases, the individual will be able to review the evidence that they have gathered and reflect on the number of times their predictions were accurate. It is hoped that the individual begins to realise that their fears were based more on how they felt in the feared situation rather than how they actually came across.

Survey method

In the survey method, the social phobic and therapist develop a set of questions to test out specific concerns about their feared symptoms. For example, they may ask someone what they think about an individual showing signs of anxiety (e.g., blushing). This is often a useful way for the individual to learn that the experience of some anxiety is entirely normal and that other people don't interpret their social behaviour as negatively as they think they do. The survey can be conducted either by the individual or the therapist, in person or perhaps via email or other format. It can be completed by family, friends or even just people in the street. The hope is that in doing this the individual is able to disconfirm their social fears by finding out that everyone experiences anxiety, and that most people do not judge others harshly or reject them for displaying symptoms of anxiety or performing less well in social situations.

(5) *Dealing with anticipatory and post-event processing*
The treatment of social phobia using this approach also includes targeting the before and after the event processing. Individuals are asked to think about the particular ways in which they think and act both before and after feared social situations. The advantages and disadvantages of their thoughts and behaviours are discussed and it is hoped that the individual will come to learn that the disadvantages predominate and that they actually just makes things worse.

(6) *Planning for the future*
Throughout their therapy, an individual with social phobia will have gathered a lot of information about their disorder, such as completed thought records (i.e., written records of one's thoughts, feelings or actions in a given situation or context), surveys or behavioural experiments. It is

useful to reflect then on what they have learnt about their phobia and create a summary. This summary will capture all the reasons underpinning the start of their phobia and what maintained it, what the main fears were and what they ultimately discovered about the validity of those fears. A plan for the future could also be included covering what they should do over the next few months as well as a plan for any set-back they might encounter.

Does CBT based on the cognitive model for social phobia work?

To date, there have been a number of studies that have examined whether therapy based on the principles outlined in the cognitive model of social phobia is effective. The first trial of this therapy was based in the UK and concentrated on generalised social phobia. The therapy was compared with:

- drug treatment (fluoxetine, which is an anti-depressant)
- self-exposure and **placebo**
- self-exposure

Whilst all three treatments brought about positive improvements for the individuals in the study, the therapy was the most effective compared to the other two types (Clark et al., 2003).

Other studies have looked at the success of the therapy depending on whether it was delivered in an individual or group format. For example, Stangier et al. (2003) recruited 71 individuals with social phobia into their study, with 65 completing the post-treatment assessment and 59 completing a 6-month follow-up. Measures of social phobia revealed a significant improvement from pre-treatment to post-treatment for both the individual and group format. However, they found that the individual therapy was better than the group format on several measures, both after the treatment had finished and again at the 6-month follow-up. This suggests then that the best way to treat social phobics using therapy is to do it as a one-to-one programme.

Other psychological treatments

Apart from CBT, there are other treatment options available when trying to treat someone with social phobia and these include: exposure therapy, exposure role plays and social skills training.

Exposure to feared situations

This technique (see Chapter 3 for a review), which is also called *in vivo* **exposure**, involves confronting a feared situation repeatedly, until the situation no longer causes anxiety or fear. For example, someone who identifies talking to people of authority as a fearful situation might purposefully go to a professor and ask questions about homework, or go to a pharmacist and ask questions about medication he or she is taking. Exposure works best when it occurs frequently (e.g., several times per week), and when it lasts long enough for the fear to decrease (up to two hours). Whilst this form of treatment may be effective for some individuals, overall the benefit to patients may be modest. For example, Heimberg et al. (1990) reported that only 65 per cent of patients being treated in this way experienced 'clinically significant improvement'. There are many different definitions of what a 'clinically significant improvement' might be (e.g., that a score in the range of a dysfunctional population at pre-treatment should fall within the range of a normal population after treatment; Jacobson et al., 1984). The important point to make here is that it shouldn't just be that participants fare better after treatment (compared to controls) but that they should be reporting and displaying scores that indicate *a clinical improvement in terms of their social phobia.*

Exposure role plays

Role plays are similar to the exposure practices described above, except that they are simulated practices instead of practising the real thing. For example, someone who is anxious about going to a job interview might practise a simulated interview with a friend, family member or therapist. When the role play practices become easier, the individual may then move on to practice exposure in the real situation. The advantage of this method is that it can help the patient build up to the 'real event'.

Social skills training

After avoiding certain social situations for an extended time, it is not surprising that some people with social anxiety disorder might develop some bad habits in social situations, including making poor eye contact and engaging in other anxious behaviours. They may also find it difficult to think of what to say during a conversation or date. Or, they may lack certain basic public speaking skills. If this is the case, CBT may include social skills training as a component. Examples include teaching an individual how to make the best impression during a job interview, how to be more assertive and how to use non-verbal communication (e.g., body language, eye contact) more effectively.

Biological treatments

The alternative option for the treatment of social phobia is that of drug treatment. There are a number of reasons as to why drug treatment might be used. For example, the individual with social phobia might prefer this type of intervention (i.e., it does not involve interaction with others), psychological intervention (such as CBT outlined previously) might have failed or there may indeed be a very lengthy wait for psychological therapy or perhaps there is a significant **co-morbidity** with depression.

In recent years there have been a number of studies that have looked at whether social phobia can be treated successfully using drugs. Indeed, the evidence suggests that a number of powerful medications that are highly effective in the acute treatment of the disorder can be used. In particular, **selective serotonin reuptake inhibitors (SSRIs)** have proven to be a particularly popular drug treatment (Blanco et al., 2003; Davidson, 2003). SSRIs were initially developed for the treatment of depression but clinicians noticed that these drugs also had anti-anxiety effects and this prompted researchers to examine whether they could be helpful in the treatment of social phobia. Since then, a number of studies that have included various types of SSRIs have been conducted, and paroxetine is one of the most studied. For example, Leibowitz et al. (2002) randomised 384 patients who met the DSM-IV criteria for social phobia into a study which compared paroxetine (either 20, 40 or 60 mg) once a day for 12 weeks with a **placebo**. It was found that patients treated with paroxetine (20 mg a day) had a significantly greater improvement on scores on the Leibowitz Social Anxiety Scale (see earlier in the chapter for description of this scale). Indeed, there have been several trials of various SSRIs including sertraline, paroxetine, fluvoxamine and citalopram and, overall, they appear to be particularly effective in the treatment of social phobia.

However, whilst it may appear that drug treatments are highly effective, it should be noted that approximately half of patients will relapse (i.e., their symptoms will re-appear) when the drug treatment is stopped, and so it is usual for treatment to last for at least 12 months.

Future directions

Little is known about how successful a combination of both psychological intervention, such as cognitive behavioural therapy, and drug treatments might be, and this is one area for future researchers to examine. Finally, it is also worth remembering that treatment will depend a lot on patient preference, motivation and availability of psychological therapy. However, like many other anxiety disorders, CBT is a popular choice and is usually more acceptable to individuals and has a reduced risk of relapse (Wells & Clark, 1995).

Section summary

In this section, we have learnt about different types of treatments available to help those living with social phobia. In particular, treatment based on the cognitive model has proven especially popular.

◉ Chapter Summary

In this chapter we have explored social phobia, a phobia which can be a debilitating disorder that may lead to a number of personal and social challenges and which can manifest its symptoms in a number of ways, such as fear, avoidance as well as physiological symptoms (e.g., blushing or sweating). Whilst it appears to be more common in females, and begins in adolescence, the precise cause of this disorder is hard to pin down, given the many different factors associated with it. However, the cause of social phobia is likely to be the result of a complex interplay between genetic and environmental factors. As our understanding of social phobia has grown, so too has our ability to diagnose, measure and treat it. As we have seen, there are broadly two types of treatments: psychological and drug treatments. We have considered how CBT can be used to treat social phobia and in particular, the influential work of Clark & Wells, who developed the cognitive model of social phobia. The general consensus appears to be that CBT based on this cognitive model is effective in the treatment of those living with social phobia; however, there is still more research needed particularly in relation to treatments which employ a combination of psychological therapy and drug treatment. In the next chapter, we will focus on agoraphobia.

◉ Further reading

Hofman, S.G. & Otto, M.W. (2008) *Cognitive-Behavioral Therapy of Social Anxiety Disorder: Evidence-Based and Disorder-Specific Treatment Techniques*. London: Routledge.

Key search terms

Social phobia; social anxiety; cognitive behavioural therapy.

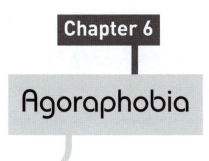

Chapter 6

Agoraphobia

👁 Introduction

Agoraphobia is an anxiety disorder that is often characterised by a fear of
having a panic attack in a public setting from which there is no straightforward or easy means of escape. People with agoraphobia are likely to
experience a cluster of phobias and generally will find it challenging or
indeed impossible to undertake certain activities. For example, agoraphobics may find it difficult to go out in public, use a lift or take public
transport.

In this chapter, we focus on agoraphobia and its historical background
through to its current definition. As this chapter will describe, it is often
associated with panic disorder and panic attacks, and so any discussion
of agoraphobia must include discussion of these other disorders also and
this book is no exception. In order to do this, methodological as well as
diagnostic issues are discussed and key debates identified. Having done
this, we will consider who suffers from agoraphobia before we turn our
attention to some of the common explanations for the development of
agoraphobia as well as treatment approaches and outcomes. As we will
see, this disorder is not nearly as straightforward as other disorders or
phobias, and so the chapter aims to present more of a summary of what
we have learnt so far and also identifies some of the challenges that have
troubled researchers and practitioners in the field.

In this chapter, we will
- Describe agoraphobia, including its relationship with panic disorder and panic attacks
- Identify some of the challenges in understanding agoraphobia
- Consider a range of possible causes of agoraphobia
- Discuss different types of treatments and how effective they are

Historical background

In 1871, a German physician Westphal described a disorder in which, he considered, the most important features as anxiety when out walking in open places or crossing streets which were empty. He suggested the name 'agoraphobia', which comes from the Greek word *agora* (which means marketplace) and *phobia* (from the Greek word phobos which means flight or terror), that is a fear of the marketplace (Mathews et al., 1981). His paper described the experiences of three patients all with similar features or symptoms. For example, they experienced anxiety under certain situations such as crossing an open space or street, in churches or in places where there were quite a number of people together. He described how they would experience heat sensations, palpitations, blushing and trembling. In addition, he described anticipatory anxiety, a fear of dying and a concern about drawing attention to oneself, when they experienced this anxiety. He also noted how this anxiety could subside under certain situations, for example, when a friend was present, or when a conversation is distracting or when drinking alcohol.

What is agoraphobia?

The precise definition of agoraphobia and its description within the DSM has changed over the years. When the DSM-III was produced in 1980, the label 'phobic disorders' was included and, under this label, we found agoraphobia along with social phobia and simple phobia (now known as specific phobia in more recent versions of DSM). Of particular interest was the fact that agoraphobia also included the specification, *with or without panic attacks* (see Box 6.1 for a description of panic attacks).

Box 6.1: What are panic attacks?

Panic attacks can be characterised by:

A discrete period of intense fear or discomfort, in the absence of real danger, that is accompanied by at least 4 of 13 somatic or cognitive symptoms (as outlined by DSM-IV-TR). Symptoms can be somatic or cognitive in nature and include palpitations, sweating, trembling or shaking, sensations of shortness of breath or smothering, feelings of choking, chest pain or discomfort, nausea or abdominal distress, dizziness or lightheadedness, derealization or depersonalisation, fear of losing control or 'going crazy', fear of dying, parasthesias (i.e., a sensation of tingling, pricking or numbness), and chills or hot flushes. The attack has a sudden onset and builds up to a peak rapidly (usually 10 minutes or less) and is often accompanied by a sense of imminent danger or impending doom, and urge to escape (APA, 2000, p. 430).

Further, panic attacks can then be described as unexpected or uncued, in that they aren't linked to a clearly identifiable trigger event. These attacks are seen as coming from nowhere, out of the blue as it were, as opposed to those which are defined by happening, almost always, immediately on exposure to, or in anticipation of, a specific situational cue or trigger. Finally, the term 'limited-symptom attacks' is used when less than four symptoms are present.

The revision of DSM-III to DSM-III-R (APA, 1987) found agoraphobia becoming a *secondary* feature of panic disorder and, therefore, is under the label 'anxiety states'. Two categories were included in this revision: (1) *panic disorder with agoraphobia* and (2) *panic disorder without agoraphobia*. Under 'phobic disorders', the category *agoraphobia without panic attacks* was included. In the DSM-IV (APA, 1994), these three labels were also found, but all located under the label 'anxiety disorders'.

Agoraphobia, according to the DSM, is marked by the following key characteristics:

- Anxiety about being in places or situations from which escape might be difficult (or embarrassing) or in which help may not be available in the event of having an unexpected or situationally predisposed panic attack or panic-like symptoms. Agoraphobic fears typically involve characteristic clusters of situations that include being outside the home alone; being in a crowd or standing in a queue; being on a bridge; and travelling on a bus, train, or in an automobile.

- The situations are avoided (e.g., travel is restricted) or else endured with marked distress or with anxiety about having a panic attack or panic-like symptoms, or require the presence of a companion.
- The anxiety of phobic avoidance is not better accounted for by another mental disorder, such as social phobia (e.g., avoidance limited to social situations because of fear of embarrassment), specific phobia (e.g., avoidance limited to a single situation like elevators), obsessive-compulsive disorder (e.g., avoiding getting dirty by someone with an obsession about contamination), post-traumatic stress disorder (e.g., avoiding stimuli associated with a severe stressor) or separation anxiety (e.g., avoiding leaving home or relatives).

From this, the diagnostic definitions of each of the three disorders outlined previously are made up of combinations of the above characteristics:

Panic disorder without agoraphobia: This diagnosis is defined by the presence of recurrent unexpected panic attacks and that one of the attacks has been followed by (1) persistent concerns about having additional attacks or (2) worry about the implications of the attack or its consequences or (3) a significant change in behaviour related to attacks. For this diagnosis, the absence of agoraphobia is required.

Panic disorder with agoraphobia: This diagnosis uses the same criteria as above, apart from the fact that the presence of agoraphobia is required.

Agoraphobia without panic attacks: This diagnosis is based on the presence of agoraphobia and is related to panic-like symptoms like dizziness or diarrhea, but panic disorder as defined above is not present. In addition, if a medical condition is present, then the fear must exceed that which is normally associated with this medical condition.

Of interest is the fact that with each revision to DSM we have seen agoraphobia being gradually relegated to secondary importance. That is to say, its presence is seen as residual to panic disorder and panic attacks. In addition, the DSM-IV-TR definition of agoraphobia is really rather different from the definition used in other phobic disorders. Specifically, the diagnostic criteria for agoraphobia are linked not only to the concept of panic attacks and panic disorder but also to 'panic-like symptoms' (i.e., agoraphobia without history of panic disorder). Why is this so? The reason for the changes in the DSM criteria is related to the fact that across studies, using clinical samples, agoraphobic patients with no history of panic disorder or panic-like symptoms appear to be very rare indeed. Fava et al. (2008) suggest that this has resulted, in part, through an inherent bias in the diagnostic and assessment tools towards the temporally causal role of panic attacks or panic-like symptoms. As a result, it is argued that it is almost impossible to diagnose agoraphobia outwith the context of panic disorder or panic-like symptoms. Understanding agoraphobia is a complex task and there are a number of key issues which have proven to be controversial and contributed to the seemingly contradictory literature on this disorder (see Box 6.2).

Box 6.2: Key debates in the agoraphobia field

Whilst there is little, if any, debate within the field about the diagnostic criteria for *panic disorder (and panic attacks)*, or the fact that both are related to agoraphobia, there is still much controversy surrounding the following key issues:

(1) Does agoraphobia exist at all, independent of panic disorder and panic-like symptoms?

(2) Are panic attacks (or panic-like symptoms) always causally linked to agoraphobia?

(3) Is there any clinical benefit of diagnosing agoraphobia as a distinct and separate disorder?

(4) How, if at all, can we define and specify criteria for agoraphobia better?

How common is agoraphobia?

On the face of it, this should be a relatively straightforward question; however, the changes in the DSM mean that different studies over time have used slightly different methods to assess prevalence rates. Nevertheless, despite some small differences between studies, there is a fair amount of consistency that suggests that the rates for agoraphobia without history of panic attacks are at least as high, if not higher than those for panic disorder.

In a recent review by Faravelli et al. (2009), it was found that 46 to 85 per cent of participants, across five **epidemiological** studies, had agoraphobia without panic attacks. In contrast, when considering the findings of clinical studies, the prevalence of agoraphobia without panic attacks was much lower (ranging from 0 to 31 per cent).

Changes in the definition of agoraphobia – in terms of prevalence

If we look at the evidence from studies published since the 1990s, we must bear in mind that there were changes in how agoraphobia was defined. For example, the DSM stipulated that there had to be a 'cluster' of situations, which means there had to be at least two agoraphobic situations reported in order to have a diagnosis of agoraphobia. As a consequence, the 12 month rate (the number of individuals in a 12-month period in a specific population who have suffered from a disorder) for agoraphobia without panic attacks was 1.3 per cent.

What is also important to recognise is that the apparent differences in prevalence rates that we have observed across studies and over time may be attributed to methodological and assessment differences (including the more recent stricter criteria for agoraphobia). What this means is that we now see *more* cases of panic disorder without agoraphobia than panic disorder with agoraphobia.

Which comes first – the chicken or the egg?

There have been a number of studies that have explored the timeline associated with panic disorder, panic attacks and agoraphobia. In particular, researchers have been keen to determine whether panic or panic-like symptoms *always* come before the onset of agoraphobia? The majority of the evidence has not found any support for this and has revealed that many agoraphobics had never experienced any panic attacks or panic-like symptoms that came before agoraphobic avoidance behaviour (e.g. Eaton & Keyl, 1990). If they did, then this usually came after the onset of agoraphobia. Overall, from the longitudinal research in this area, panic attacks are just as likely to come before agoraphobia as they come after it (Wittchen et al., 2010).

Gender and age of onset

The evidence suggests a greater prevalence of agoraphobia without history of panic disorders for females (see Box 6.3), than that for the ones with panic disorder (Goodwin et al., 2005; Perugi et al., 2007). The extent to which gender and age of onset are together related to panic disorder and agoraphobia remains somewhat unclear; however, there have been several studies that have examined age of onset for panic attacks as well as panic disorders both with and without agoraphobia. Overall, the evidence appears to be fairly consistent (Wittchen et al., 2010). In general, age of onset appears to be in the early twenties (Kessler et al., 2006); however, some studies do suggest slightly higher ages, but this is almost certainly due to differences in the samples. The evidence thus far suggests that for panic disorder, approximately two-thirds of cases will develop before the age of 35 years. With regard to panic attacks, the evidence suggests two important time points (i.e., 15 to 19 years; 35 to 50) where these are likely to develop. Unfortunately, however, the picture with regard to agoraphobia panic attacks is less clear. Some studies have reported that 25 to 29 as the average age of onset, whereas other studies argue for a second peak around the age of 40 (De Graaf et al., 2003; Eaton et al., 1991; Wittchen et al., 1992).

Other socio-demographic associations

To date, there has been little evidence of any consistent association between socio-demographic factors with any of the three disorders, apart from one key finding, which is, individuals who have *agoraphobia without panic attacks* as well as those affected by *panic disorder with agoraphobia* are more likely to be unemployed and disabled as compared to individuals living with *panic disorder without agoraphobia* (Kessler et al., 2005; Wittchen et al., 1998).

Box 6.3: What accounts for the gender difference?

If we think about possible reasons as to why there appears to be a gender difference in the prevalence of agoraphobia, then we need to reflect on the processes through which we come to identify individuals with such a disorder. For example, in order for an individual to be diagnosed with an illness they need to seek help and report their symptoms to a health professional. However, could there be a difference between males and females in the extent to which they seek help when living with agoraphobia (and its symptoms)? If so, it may explain the gender difference in prevalence rates?

Indeed, this notion was discussed by Bekker (1996) who suggested three key reasons why there may be biases in the extent to which males and females share their experiences of agoraphobia:

- The traditional masculine sex-role stereotypes may make it harder for males to be open about their feelings and any anxiety they have, including symptoms of agoraphobia.
- The relationship between sex-role stereotypes and the specific use of alcohol as a coping mechanism may also be relevant. For example, an excessive use of alcohol may lead to problems and a diagnosis of alcoholism, but those may mask the seriousness of any agoraphobic symptoms.
- It is thought that gender roles with regard to avoidance-related behaviour may also help to explain prevalence rates. For example, within Western culture men are more likely to be the breadwinners and likely to have jobs that take them outside their home. It is suggested that as females are more likely to be housewives; this may create a situation in which there is a tendency to avoid going outside.

Impact of these disorders

To date, there have not been many studies that have examined the impact of these various disorders on the individual. However, from the available evidence we see an emerging picture. That is to say, impairment and disability appear to be greatest for those with *panic disorder with agoraphobia* compared to those with *panic disorder without agoraphobia* or *agoraphobia without panic attacks*. However, for all those who live with these problems, there is clearly an impact on everyday life and functioning as illustrated by the case studies in Box 6.4.

Box 6.4: Some examples of people living with agoraphobia

Michelle is 22 years old and has recently started a new job in the city centre. However, in order to get there she has to travel on a busy bus into town then walk to her office, crossing several roads. She finds the trip to work something of an ordeal and has become very anxious about doing it on her own. Sometimes her boyfriend accompanies her to work and this makes her feel a little better, though she remains still anxious but not as bad.

Dave is 47 and has been scared of open spaces for over a decade. He is unable to go out with his two children to the park or football matches. If Dave goes out he fears he is going to collapse through stress or have a heart attack. This fear grips him and even the anticipation of going outside can lead him to become extremely anxious.

Co-morbidity

Evidence suggests that *panic disorder with agoraphobia* (52 per cent) and *agoraphobia with panic attacks* (52.3 per cent) have higher co-morbidity rates compared with that for *agoraphobia without panic attacks* (33.1 per cent) (Wittchen et al., 2010). In relation to other anxiety disorders, co-morbidities are found to be in a similar range (49–64 per cent) for all three groups, however, *agrophobia without panic attacks* appeared to be more co-morbid, compared with other phobic disorders (Wittchen et al., 2010). Overall, the emerging literature appears to suggest that agoraphobia is most likely to be associated with other anxiety disorders and phobias, whereas panic attacks and panic disorder are linked to a far-broader range of comorbid conditions.

Clinical course and remission

When researchers have looked at the clinical course of both panic disorder and agoraphobia, the picture emerges of a chronic and recurrent set of problems. For example, in a study by Emmelkamp & Wittchen (2009), *agoraphobia without panic attacks* was found to be one of the more persistent problems over a 10-year follow-up period. Indeed, the picture is even more gloomy as they also found that cases of full remission were very rare indeed. In fact, nobody in their sample, who was living with agoraphobia, had experienced complete **remission**.

In addition, the presence of severe agoraphobia has been shown to be one of the most important predictors of long-term outcome of panic disorder. For example, in a follow-up study of panic disorder with agoraphobia, which was treated by exposure, the presence of residual agoraphobia was found to predict the chances of relapse into panic (Fava et al., 2001).

◉ What causes agoraphobia?

In a similar way to social phobia (see Chapter 5), there has been a considerable body of work that has examined the causes of panic disorder, panic disorder with agoraphobia as well as agoraphobia without panic attacks. Again, there are a variety of factors that may explain the development of these problems and, broadly, they fall into the following two main types:

Psychological/Environmental explanations

- Past experiences
- Family factors

Biological explanations

- Genetic factors

Often when we explore the causes of illness, we forget that those living with a disorder may well have ideas of their own as to what caused it (we explore this further in Box 6.5).

Psychological/environmental explanations

Past experiences

There is evidence to suggest that traumatic or negative events in childhood (e.g., separation or death of parent) are linked to both agoraphobia and panic disorder (Kessler et al., 1997; Peter et al., 2005). Indeed, this finding is consistent with other evidence suggesting that a greater number of past negative life events are associated with increased likelihood of various disorders. It appears to be the case that it is the *number* of life events which is important, rather than the exact type of event.

Family factors

Across a number of studies, the role of family climate and child-rearing behaviour has been examined in relation to panic disorder and agoraphobia. More specifically, 'reduced warmth' and 'overprotection' have been shown to be important, particularly in relation to panic disorder

(Aoki et al., 1994; Laraia et al., 1994). There appears to be less attention given to exploring the link between *agoraphobia without panic attacks* and family climate.

A psychological explanation for the maintenance of agoraphobia: The cognitive model

In the previous chapter we explored the cognitive model of social phobia and also how this has helped shape psychological treatments. Similarly, the development of agoraphobia has also been explained in cognitive terms, with the role of **threat appraisal** and related anxiety behaviours being considered as particularly relevant. The cognitive explanation for agoraphobia suggests that anxiety in a specific situation may be elevated unnecessarily if the individual perceives there to be danger and/or they do not believe they could cope with the danger. This perception of the level of danger in a situation or their ability to cope will be shaped by their pre-existing negative beliefs.

In the case of panic disorder, the individual has a tendency to misperceive certain bodily sensations as an indication of impending danger. As a result, the individual may pay selective attention to certain threat-related stimuli in their social environment as well as view any physiological arousal as evidence of imminent danger. In addition, they may engage in safety-seeking behaviours, which might include avoidance behaviour. Such avoidance behaviours are particularly important as they prevent the individual from experiencing a situation that disconfirms their negative beliefs about the danger present. That is, if the individual always avoids going outside then they are unable to learn that in fact the level of danger was grossly over-estimated. As panic and avoidance behaviours continue the problem becomes more habitual and any awareness that there is a cognitive component to the cycle declines.

Agoraphobia, according to the cognitive model, may well be related to panic disorder but it needn't be (Salkovskis & Hackman, 1997). In general, agoraphobics believe that entering a specific situation is likely to result in some serious harm or emotional distress. However, their appraisal of the danger is not justified in the sense that the harm seldom, if at all, materialises. It is evident then from this cognitive explanation that belief change ought to be at the heart of any psychological treatment.

Box 6.5: What do patients think caused their agoraphobia?

Within the literature, there has been comparatively little attention given to understanding what patients' believe has caused their anxiety disorder, such as agoraphobia. However, one interesting study by Wardle et al. (1997) explored the beliefs of patients who were being recruited into an agoraphobia treatment trial. Patients were asked to rate the contribution of eight factors in causing their disorder. In addition, they were asked to select the *major cause* of their agoraphobia and this was evaluated in relation to their **attributional style**. The most common cause, from the patient's perspective, was that of *stress*, which also had the highest average ratings. Following this were patient's reported *disposition* (i.e., being a naturally nervous person), *circumstances* (staying home too much) and childhood experiences.

Biological explanations

Genetic factors

There appears to be higher incidence of first-degree relatives of those with panic disorder also suffering from the same condition. Indeed, Hayward et al. (2004) argue that parental history of *panic disorder with agoraphobia* may have a central role in the development of panic attacks in offspring. However, as Wittchen et al. (2010) point out, this argument should be treated with caution since panic attacks and panic disorder are related to increased incidence of a broad range of disorders (Biederman et al., 2006; Lieb et al., 2000). That said, there does appear to be at least some unique genetic contribution to *panic disorder with agoraphobia* (Biederman et al., 2001; Crowe et al., 1983; Weissman, 1993). Whether there is an increased risk of developing *panic disorder*, *panic disorder with agoraphobia* and *agoraphobia without panic attacks*, remains unclear. In one study by Harris et al. (1983), there was an increased risk for both *panic disorder* and *agoraphobia without panic attacks*. However, Smeraldi et al. (1989) found that this increased risk was specific to agoraphobia.

Section summary

In this section we have considered the nature of agoraphobia and its relationship with panic attacks and panic disorders. As we have seen, there are a number of possible explanations for the development of agoraphobia and, as we have seen, there are a number of key issues for debate in this area. Next, we turn our attention to the treatment of agoraphobia.

Treatment of agoraphobia

As we saw in Chapter 5, both psychological and drug treatment have proven to be the two most popular types of intervention. Given the complex inter-relationships that exist between panic disorder, panic attacks and agoraphobia, together with changes in definition and diagnostic tools, there has been some confusion in the field as to what is the most effective treatment (or indeed combination of treatments). In this section, we shall attempt to try and draw together and summarise the main findings that have emerged.

To date, we have seen many studies that have reported **Cognitive Behavioural Therapy** (see Chapter 5) and anti-depressants as being the two most effective types of treatment for panic disorder with agoraphobia (McHugh et al., 2009). However, there has been considerable debate in the field as to which of these treatment options is *more* effective. Similarly, is there a benefit from combining these treatment options for individuals? One way to examine this issue is to look to studies which are **meta-analyses** of studies in the field. The findings of some of these meta-analytical studies have suggested that improvement for panic disorder with agoraphobia is greater for cognitive behavioural therapy when used *alone* than from either drug treatment or when combined with psychological treatment. However, these findings have been criticised as being flawed on methodological grounds and so the jury is still out on this one (Kelin, 2000). Exposure *in vivo* has proven to be a popular choice of treatment for agoraphobia, particularly since the early 1980s. A common exposure *in vivo* treatment encourages the individual to approach feared situations in a graduated way and to remain in them until the anxiety subsides. Whilst there is a sizeable body of literature that suggests this approach is effective (Wittchen et al., 2010), there are some difficulties when assessing treatment studies conducted using the dated DSM-III criteria (as noted earlier). Similarly, there have been difficulties in assessing the efficacy of drug treatment on agoraphobia as a result of this issue, and there is a lack of up to date controlled trials.

 Chapter Summary

In this chapter we have explored agoraphobia, a disorder that can have a profound impact on the lives of those who suffer from it. At the heart of the disorder is the fear of having a panic attack in a public setting, from which there is no straightforward or easy means of escape. People with agoraphobia are likely to experience a cluster of phobias and generally will find it challenging or indeed impossible to undertake certain activities. However, we have also seen that agoraphobia is intimately linked with panic disorder and panic attacks, and according to DSM-IV-TR, is not a condition in its own right but rather secondary to panic disorder or panic-like symptoms. As we have seen, this is a highly controversial issue and the evidence we have is further complicated by changes in the definition of and criteria used to classify the presence of agoraphobia. There are also a number of potential explanations for agoraphobia, though the issues mentioned previously are also relevant to the study of its aetiology. In terms of treatment, both psychological and drug treatments have been common, with exposure *in vivo* a popular and effective choice. In summary, this is a complex disorder with much debate surrounding it within the scientific literature. The present chapter has sought to provide a useful, albeit brief, summary of the key issues and findings.

Further reading

Silove, D. & Manicavasagar, V. (2009) *Overcoming Panic and Agoraphobia*. Robinson Publishing, London.

Key search terms

Agoraphobia; agoraphobia without panic attacks, panic disorder.

Glossary

adjunctive therapy treatment used together with the primary treatment, the purpose being to assist the primary treatment.

agoraphobia severe and pervasive anxiety about being in situations from which escape might be difficult; or avoidance of situations such as being alone outside of the home, travelling in a car, bus or airplane, or being in a crowded area (DSM-IV).

agoraphobic avoidance a safety-seeking behaviour undertaken by an individual who is fearful of the harmful consequences of a certain situation or environment, for example, going outside.

amygdala an almond-shaped structure deep in the brain that is believed to be a communications hub between the parts of the brain that process incoming sensory signals and the parts that interpret these signals. It can alert the rest of the brain that a threat is present and trigger a fear or anxiety response.

anterior cingulated cortex the frontal part of the cingulate cortex that resembles a 'collar' form around the corpus callosum, the fibrous bundle that relays neural signals between the right and left cerebral hemispheres of the brain. It appears to play a role in a wide variety of autonomic functions, such as regulating blood pressure and heart rate, as well as rational cognitive functions, such as reward anticipation, decision-making, empathy and emotion.

arousal a physiological and psychological state of being awake or reactive to stimuli.

arthropods/arthropod species a biological classification that accounts for almost 80 per cent of all living species and includes animals such as insects, crustaceans and arachnids.

associative model   a 'learning' or 'conditioning' term that refers to learning that two different events occur or happen together.

attributional style   how people explain the events of their lives.

autonomic nervous system   part of the peripheral nervous system that acts as a control system functioning largely below the level of consciousness, and controls visceral functions. This affects heart rate, digestion, respiration rate, salivation, perspiration, diameter of the pupils, urination and sexual arousal. Whereas most of its actions are involuntary, some, such as breathing, work in tandem with the conscious mind.

behavioural observation   the process of viewing an individual's behaviour directly, which may also include some form of recording of behaviours.

benign   of little or no harm.

benzodiazepines   medications that slow the central nervous system to ease nervousness and tension.

biphasic reaction/response   having two distinct phases

catastrophic thinking/beliefs/cognitions   irrational thoughts or beliefs held by an individual, typically involving perceived danger or harm (i.e., the catastrophic event), though in reality the danger is unlikely to occur.

ceiling effect   when performance or functioning is nearly perfect, the existing state of near perfection is referred to as the ceiling effect – since performance is bumping into the top or roof of the scale of what can be achieved.

circumscribed   within a well-defined area. For example, circumscribed anxiety may refer to anxiety limited to only one specific object or event as in specific phobia.

classical conditioning   a form of associative learning, first demonstrated by Pavlov. The typical procedure for inducing classical conditioning involves presentations of a neutral stimulus along with a stimulus of some significance, the 'unconditioned stimulus'. The neutral stimulus could be any event that does not result in an overt behavioural response from the organism under investigation.

clinical populations   also known as 'patient population' or group of patients with a given illness or disease.

cognitive behavioural therapy/treatment   a psychotherapeutic approach, a talking therapy, that aims to solve problems concerning dysfunctional emotions, behaviours and cognitions through a goal-oriented, systematic procedure.

cognitive restructuring the process of learning to refute cognitive distortions, or fundamental 'faulty thinking', with the goal of replacing one's irrational, counter-factual beliefs with more accurate and beneficial ones.

collinearity when two or more independent variables are highly correlated.

co-morbidity (also co-morbid) a disease, disorder or condition that occurs at the same time as another disorder but is not related to it.

confederate an actor who participates in a psychological experiment pretending to be a participant but in actuality working for the researcher (also known as a 'stooge').

counterbalancing an arrangement of treatment conditions to neutralise practice effects and/or the effects of fatigue, for example, where group A completes Task 1 followed by Task 2, and group B completes Task 2 followed by Task 1.

demand characteristics used in psychology experiments to describe a cue that makes participants aware of what the experimenter expects to find or how participants are expected to behave.

Diagnostic and Statistical Manual of Mental Disorders published by the American Psychiatric Association and provides a common language and standard criteria for the classification of mental disorders.

dopamine a catecholamine neurotransmitter present in a variety of animals.

dyadic an interpersonal situation that involves another individual.

ecologically valid the extent to which research results can be applied to real-life situations outside of research settings.

epidemiological study /epidemiology the study of patterns of health and illness and associated factors at the population level. Epidemiology also provides evidence for the potential causes of health and illness/disorders.

ethics committee a committee appointed to consider ethical issues of research studies and the welfare of the human participants.

fight or flight (response) response to an acute threat to survival that is marked by physical changes, including nervous and endocrine changes, that prepare a human or an animal to react or to retreat.

galvanic skin response   a change in the ability of the skin to conduct electricity, caused by an emotional stimulus, such as the target of one's phobia or phobic stimulus.

generalised social phobia   a fear of most social interactions together with a fear of most performance situations (e.g., speaking in public).

homogeneous   of the same kind, sharing the same characteristics.

hypothalamus–pituitary gland–adrenocortical axis   a complex set of direct influences and feedback interactions among the hypothalamus, the pituitary gland (a pea-shaped structure located below the hypothalamus) and the adrenal (or suprarenal) glands (small, conical organs on top of the kidneys).

internal reliability   the extent to which a measure is consistent within itself.

in vivo **exposure**   a therapy technique in which feared situations are experienced in order to decrease anxiety.

individual difference variable   the variables that occur naturally and that a researcher cannot assign a participant to. These include gender, age, height and so on.

lifetime co-morbidity   the co-occurrence of a related disorder or illness across a lifetime.

lifetime prevalence   the number of individuals in a statistical population that at some point in their life (up to the time of assessment) have experienced a 'case' (e.g., a disorder).

maladaptive cognitions   negative, distorted or irrational thoughts

meta-analysis   combines the results of several studies that address a set of related research hypotheses. In its simplest form, this is normally by identification of a common measure of effect size, for which a weighted average might be the output of a meta-analyses.

modelling   a general process in which an individual (or individuals) serve as models for others, exhibiting the behaviour which may be imitated by the others.

natural selection   the process whereby organisms better adapted to their environment tend to survive and produce more offspring.

naturalistic study/studies   a type of study in which the researcher very carefully observes and records some behaviour or phenomenon, sometimes over a prolonged period, in its natural setting while interfering as little as possible with the participants or phenomena.

negative self-processing   the process of considering information about oneself in a negative or pessimistic way.

oedipal conflict a term used by Freud in his theory of psychosexual stages of development to describe a boy's feelings of desire for his mother, and jealously and anger towards his father.

ontogenetic relating to or based on embryonic developmental history.

operant conditioning the use of a behaviour's antecedent and/or its consequence to influence the occurrence and form of behaviour.

paradigm logical systems made up of theories and research techniques that reflect a predominant way of thinking about a particular topic.

pervasive anxiety continuous chronic anxiety of a so-called 'free floating' variety which is ever-present and intensive.

phylogenetic relating to or based on evolutionary development or history.

placebo a sham or simulated medical intervention.

post-traumatic stress disorder (PTSD) a complex anxiety disorder in which the affected person's memory, emotional responses, intellectual processes and nervous system have all been disrupted by one or more traumatic experiences.

prevalence the number of people in a given population who meet criteria for a disorder over a given time frame.

prospective design/prospective study a study design within which an individual or group of people is observed in order to determine outcomes. For example, a group of individuals might be watched over an extended period of time to observe the progression of a particular disorder or to establish if they have developed a disorder.

randomised controlled trials the most rigorous way of determining whether a cause–effect relation exists between treatment and outcome. The randomised controlled trial (RCT) is a study design in which participants are allocated at random to receive one of several clinical interventions. They are often considered to be the 'gold standard' in terms of research designs, mainly because the act of randomising patients to receive (or not receive) an intervention ensures that, on average, all other possible causes are equal between the groups.

remission the state of absence of disease activity in patients with a chronic illness, with the possibility of return of disease activity.

schema (or schemata) the mental framework that allows you to make sense of aspects of your environment.

selective serotonin reuptake inhibitors   a class of compounds typically used as anti-depressants in the treatment of depression, anxiety disorders and some personality disorders.

serotonin   is a monoamine neurotransmitter. Biochemically derived from tryptophan, serotonin is primarily found in the gastrointestinal tract, platelets and in the central nervous system of animals, including humans. It is a well-known contributor to feelings of well-being; therefore it is also known as a 'happiness hormone' despite not being a hormone.

simulated exposure   a false scenario to mimic the experience of the real event.

socio-occupational   work and employment related status.

somatic symptoms   symptoms which arise from the body as distinct from the mind.

specific social phobia   when an individual is fearful of a specific situation or a specific performance behaviour (e.g., eating in public).

threat appraisal   the estimation of the chances of encountering harm and the perceived seriousness of the harm.

wait-list control   a group that is assigned to a waiting list to receive an intervention after the treatment group does. A wait list (or waiting list) control group serves the purpose of providing an untreated comparison for the active treatment group, while at the same time allowing the wait-listed participants an opportunity to obtain the intervention at a later date.

within-participants design   an experimental design where all subjects receive all treatment conditions. Also called a repeated measures design.

References

Aartman, I.H.A., Van Everdingen, T.A., Hoogstraten, J., & Schuurs, A.H.B. (1998). Self-report measurements of dental anxiety and fear in children: A critical assessment. *Journal of Dentistry for Children*, 65, 252–258.

Abrahamsson, K.H., Berggren, U., Hallberg, L., & Carlsson, S.G. (2002a). Ambivalence in coping with dental fear and avoidance: A qualitative study. *Journal of Health Psychology*, 76, 653–664.

Abrahamsson, K.H., Berggren, U., Hallberg, L., & Carlsson, S.G. (2002b). Dental phobic patients' views of dental anxiety and experiences in dental care: A qualitative study. *Scandinavian Journal of Caring Sciences*, 16, 188–196.

Adolphs, R., Cahill, L., Schul, R., & Babinsky, R. (1997). Impaired declarative memory for emotional material following bilateral amygdala damage in humans. *Learning & Memory*, 4, 291–300.

Alonso, J., Angermeyer, M.C., Bernert, S. et al. (2004). Prevalence of mental disorders in Europe: Results from the European study of the epidemiology of mental disorders (ESEMeD) project. *Acta Psychiatrica Scandinavica*, 109(420), 21–27.

Alpers, G.W., Wilhelm, F.H., & Roth, W.T. (2005). Psychophysiological assessment during exposure in driving phobic patients. *Journal of Abnormal Psychology*, 114, 126–139.

American Psychiatric Association (APA) (1980). *Diagnostic and Statistical Manual of Mental Disorders* (3rd Ed.). Washington, DC: American Psychiatric Association.

American Psychiatric Association (APA) (1987). *Diagnostic and Statistical Manual of Mental Disorders* (3rd Ed., revised). Washington, DC: American Psychiatric Association.

American Psychiatric Association (APA) (2000). *Diagnostic and Statistical Manual of Mental Disorders* (4th Ed., text revised). Washington, DC: American Psychiatric Association.

Ansseau, M., Reggers, J., Nickels, J., & Magerus, S. (1999). Epidemiologie des troubles psychiatriques dans la province de Luxembourg. *Plate-forme de concentration Psychiatrique*. Belgium: Université de Liége.

Antony, M.M., Pickren, W.E., & Koemer, N. (2009). Historical perspectives on psychiatric classification and anxiety disorders. In D. McKay, J.S. Abramowitz, S. Taylor, & G. Asmundson. (Eds.), *Current Perspectives on the Anxiety Disorders: Implications for DSM-V and Beyond*. New York: Springer.

Antony, M.M. & Barlow, D.H. (2002). Specific phobias. In D.H. Barlow (Ed.), *Anxiety and its Disorders: The Nature and Treatment of Anxiety and Panic* (pp. 380–417). New York: Guilford Press.

Antony, M.M. & Swinson, R.P. (2000). *Phobic Disorders and Panic in Adults: A Guide to Assessment and Treatment*. Washington, DC: American Psychological Association.

Antony, M.M., Brown, T.A., & Barlow, D.H. (1997). Heterogeneity among specific phobia types in DSM-IV. *Behaviour Research & Therapy*, 35, 1089–1100.

Aoki, Y., Fujihara, S., & Kitamura, T. (1994). Panic attacks and panic disorder in a Japanese nonpatient population – epidemiology and psychosocial correlates. *Journal of Affective Disorders*, 32, 51–59.

Armfield, J.M. & Mattiske, J.K. (1996). Vulnerability representation: The role of perceived dangerousness, uncontrollability, unpredictability and disgustingness in spider fear. *Behaviour Research & Therapy*, 34, 899–909.

Armfield, J.M. (2006). Cognitive vulnerability: A model of the etiology of fear. *Clinical Psychology Review*, 26, 746–768.

Armfield, J.M. (2007a). Understanding animal fears: A comparison of the cognitive vulnerability and harm-looming models. *BMC Psychiatry*, 7, 68.

Armfield, J.M. (2007b). A preliminary investigation of the relationship of dental fear to other specific fears, general fearfulness, disgust sensitivity and harm sensitivity. *Community Dentistry & Oral Epidemiology*, 36, 128–136.

Armfield, J.M., Slade, G.D., & Spencer, A.J. (2008). Cognitive vulnerability and dental fear. *BMC Oral Health*, 8, 2.

Arntz, A., Rauner, M., & Van Den Hout, M. (1995). 'If I feel anxious, there must be danger': Ex-consequentia reasoning in inferring danger in anxiety disorders. *Behaviour Research & Therapy*, 33, 917–925.

Askew, C. & Field, A.P. (2007). Vicarious learning and the development of fears in childhood. *Behaviour Research & Therapy*, 45, 2616–2627.

Askew, C. & Field, A.P. (2008). The vicarious learning pathway to fear 40 years on. *Clinical Psychology Review*, 28, 1249–1265.

Bandura, A. (1977). *Social Learning Theory*. Englewood Cliffs, NJ: Prentice-Hall.

Beatty, M.J., Heisel, A.D., Hall, A.E., Levine, T.R., & La France, B.H. (2002). What can we learn from the study of twins about genetic and environmental influences on interpersonal affiliation, aggressiveness and social anxiety? A meta-analytic study. *Communication Monographs*, 69(1), 1–18.

Bechara, A., Tranel, D., Damasio, H., Adolphs, R., Rockland, C., & Damasio, A.R. (1995). Double dissociation of conditioning and declarative knowledge relative to the amygdala and hippocampus in humans. *Science*, 269, 1115–1118.

Beck, A.T. & Emery, G. (1985). *Anxiety Disorders and Phobias: A Cognitive Perspective*. New York: Basic Books.

Becker, E., Rinck, M., Tuke, V. et al. (2007). Epidemiology of specific phobia types: Findings from the Dresden Mental Health Study. *European Psychiatry*, 22, 69–74.

Beidel, D.C., Turner, S.M., & Morris, T.L. (2000). Behavioral treatment of childhood social phobia. *Journal of Consulting & Clinical Psychology*, 68(6), 1072–1080.

Bekker, M.H.J. (1996). Agoraphobia and gender: A review. *Clinical Psychology Review*, 16(2), 129–146.

Berger, S.M. (1962). Conditioning through vicarious instigation. *Psychological Review*, 69, 450–466.

Berggren, U. (1993). Psychosocial effects associated with dental fear in adult dental patients with avoidance behaviours. *Psychology & Health*, 8, 185–196.

Biederman, J., Hirschfeld-Becker, D.R., Rosenbaum, J.F. et al. (2001). Further evidence of association between behavioral inhibition and social anxiety in children. *American Journal of Psychiatry*, 158, 1673–1679.

Biederman, J., Petty, C., Faraone, S.V. et al. (2006). Effects of parental anxiety disorders in children at high risk for panic disorder: A controlled study. *Journal of Affective Disorders*, 94, 191–197.

Bijl, R.V., Ravelli, A., & van Zessen, G. (1998). Prevalence of psychiatric disorder in the general population: Results of the Netherlands mental health survey and incidence study (NEMESIS). *Social Psychiatry & Psychiatric Epidemiology*, 33, 587–595.

Blanco, C., Schneier, F.R., Schmidt, A., Blanco-Jerez, C.R., & Marshall, R.D. (2003). Pharmacological treatment of social anxiety disorder: A meta-analysis. *Depression & Anxiety*, 18, 29–40.

Boomsma, D., Busjahn, A., & Peltonen, L. (2002). Classical twin studies and beyond. *Nature Reviews Genetics*, 3, 872–883.

Bracha, H.S., Vega, E.M., & Vega, C.B. (2006). Posttraumatic dental-care anxiety (PTDA): Is 'dental phobia' a misnomer? *Hawaii Dental Journal*, 37(5), 17–19.

Brennan, P.F. & Fink, S.V. (1997). Health promotion, social support and computer networks. In R.L. Street, W.R. Gold, T. Manning (Eds.), *Health Promotion and Interactive Technology: Applications and Future Directions* (pp. 157–169). Mahwah, NJ: Lawrence Erlbaum Associates.

Bruch, M.A. & Heimberg, R.G. (1994). Differences in perception of parental and personal characteristics between generalized and nongeneralized social phobia. *Journal of Anxiety Disorders*, 8, 155–168.

Brunello, N., den Boer, J.A., Judd, L.L. et al. (2000). Social phobia: Diagnosis and epidemiology, neurobiology and pharmacology, comorbidity and treatment. *Journal of Affective Disorders*, 60, 61–74.

Buchanan, H. & Niven, N. (2002). Validation of a facial image scale to assess child dental anxiety. *International Journal of Paediatric Dentistry*, 12(1), 47–52.

Buchanan, H. & Niven, N. (2003). Self-report informational treatment techniques used by dentists to treat dentally anxious children: A preliminary investigation. *International Journal of Paediatric Dentistry*, 13, 9–12.

Buchanan, H. (2005). Development of a computerised dental anxiety scale for children: Validation and reliability. *British Dental Journal*, 199, 359–362.

Buchanan, H. & Coulson, N.S. (2007). Accessing dental anxiety online support groups: An exploratory qualitative study of motives and experiences. *Patient Education & Counseling*, 66, 263–269.

Buchanan, H. (2010). Assessing dental anxiety in children: The revised smiley faces program. *Child: Care, Health & Development*, 36(4), 534–538.

Buchanan, H., Coulson, N.S., & Malik, S. (2010). Health-related internet support groups and dental anxiety: The fearful patient's online journey. *International Journal of Web Based Communities*, 6(4), 362–375.

Cannon, W.B. (1927). The James-Lange theory of emotions: A critical examination and an alternative. *American Journal of Psychology*, 39, 106–124.

Carrigan, M.H. & Randall, C.L. (2003). Self-medication in social phobia: A review of the alcohol literature. *Addictive Behaviors*, 28(2), 269–284.

Choy, Y., Fyer, A.J., & Lipsitz, J.D. (2007). Treatment of specific phobia in adults. *Clinical Psychology Review*, 27, 266–286.

Clark, D.M. & Wells, A. (1995). A cognitive model of social phobia. In R.G. Heimberg, M.R. Liebowitz, D.A. Hope, & F.R. Schneier (Eds.), *Social Phobia: Diagnosis, Assessment and Treatment* (pp. 69–93). New York: Guilford Press.

Clark, D.M., Ehlers, A., McManus, F., Hackman, A., Fennell, M., Campbell, H., Flower, T., Davenport, C., & Louis, B. (2003). Cognitive therapy versus fluoxetine in generalized social phobia: A randomized placebo-controlled trial. *Journal of Consulting & Clinical Psychology*, 71(6), 1058–1067.

Clark, D.M., Ehlers, A., Hackmann, A., McManus, F., Fennell, M., Grey, N., Waddington, L., & Wild, J. (2006). Cognitive therapy versus exposure and applied relaxation in social phobia: A randomised controlled trial. *Journal of Consulting & Clinical Psychology*, 73, 568–578.

Cochrane, A., Barnes-Holmes, D., & Barnes-Holmes, Y. (2008). The perceived-threat behavioural approach test (PT-BAT): Measuring avoidance in high-, mid-, and low-spider-fearful participants. *The Psychological Record*, 58, 585–596.

Coelho, C.M. & Purkis, H. (2009). The origins of specific phobia: Influential theories and current perspectives. *Review of General Psychology*, 13(4), 335–348.

Coelho, C.M., Waters, A.M., Hine, T.J., & Wallis, G. (2009). The use of virtual reality in acrophobia research and treatment. *Journal of Anxiety Disorders*, 23(5), 563–574.

Cohen, S.M., Fiske, J., & Newton, J.T. (2000). The impact of dental anxiety on daily living. *British Dental Journal*, 189, 85–90.

Connor, K.M., Davidson, J.R.T., Churchill, L.E., Sherwood, A., & Weisler, R.H. (2000). Psychometric properties of the Social Phobia Inventory (SPIN). *The British Journal of Psychiatry*, 176, 379–386.

Cook, M. & Mineka, S. (1989). Observational conditioning of fear relevant versus fear-irrelevant stimuli in rhesus monkeys. *Journal of Abnormal Psychology*, 98, 448–459.

Corah, N.L., O'Shea, R.M., & Skeels, D.K. (1982). Dentists' perceptions of problem behaviours in patients. *The Journal of the American Dental Association*, 104, 829–833.

Coulson, N.S. (2005). Receiving social support online: An analysis of a computer- mediated support group for individuals living with Irritable Bowel Syndrome. *CyberPsychology & Behaviour*, 8, 580–584.

Coulson, N.S. & Buchanan, H. (2008). Self-reported efficacy of an online dental anxiety support group: A pilot study. *Community Dentistry & Oral Epidemiology*, 36, 43–46.

Craske, M.G., Miller, P.P., Rotunda, R., & Barlow, D.H. (1990). A descriptive report of features of initial unexpected panic attacks in minimal and extensive avoiders. *Behaviour Research & Therapy*, 28, 395–400.

Craske, M.G. (2003). *Origins of Phobias and Anxiety Disorders: Why More Women than Men?* Oxford: Elsevier.

Crawford, A.N., Hawker, B.J., & Lennon, M.A. (1997). A dental support group for anxious patients. *British Dental Journal*, 183, 57–62.

Crowe, R.R., Noyes, R., Pauls, D.L., & Sylmen, D. (1983). A family study of panic disorder. *Archives of General Psychiatry*, 40, 1065–1069.

Curtis, G., Magee, W., Eaton, W. et al. (1998). Specific fears and phobias: Epidemiology and classification. *British Journal of Psychiatry*, 173, 212–217.

Cuthbert, M.I. & Melamed, B.G. (1982). A screening device: Children at risk for dental fears and management problems. *Journal of Dentistry for Children*, 49, 432–436.

Dailey, Y.M., Humphris, G.M., & Lennon, M.A. (2001).The use of dental anxiety questionnaires: A survey of a group of UK dental practitioners. *British Dental Journal*, 190(8), 450–453.

Darwin, C. (1877). A biographical sketch of an infant, *Mind*, 2, 285–294.

Davey, G.C.L. (1989). Dental phobias and anxieties – evidence for conditioning processes in the acquisition and modulation of a learned fear. *Behaviour Research & Therapy*, 27(1), 51–58.

Davidson, J.R.T., Hughes, D.L., George, L.K., & Blazer, D.G. (1993).The epidemiology of social phobia: findings from the Duke epidemiological catchment area study. *Psychological Medicine*, 23, 709–718.

Davidson, J.R.T., Miner,C.M., De Veaugh-Geiss, J., Tupler, L.A., Colket, J.T., & Potts, N.L.S. (1997). The brief social phobia scale: A psychometric evaluation. *Psychological Medicine*, 27, 161–166.

Davidson, J.R.T. (2003). Pharmacotherapy of social phobia. *Acta Psychiatrica Scandinavica*, 108, 65–71.

Degonda, M. & Angst, J. (1993). The Zurich Study XX. Social phobia and agoraphobia. *European Archives of Psychiatry & Clinical Neuroscience*, 243, 95–102.

De Graaf, R., Bijl, R.V., Spijker, J., Beckman, A.T.F., & Vollebergh, W.A.M. (2003). Temporal sequencing of lifetime mood disorders in relation to comorbid anxiety and substance use disorders: Findings from the Netherlands mental health survey and incidence survey. *Social Psychiatry & Psychiatric Epidemiology*, 38, 1–11.

De Jongh, A., Muris, P., Ter Horst, G., & Duyx, M.P.M.A. (1995). Acquisition and maintenance of dental anxiety: The role of conditioning experiences and cognitive factors. *Behaviour Research & Therapy*, 33, 205–210.

De Jongh, A., Bongaarts, G., Vermeule, I. et al. (1998). Blood–injury injection phobia and dental phobia. *Behaviour Research & Therapy*, 36, 971–982.

De Jongh, A., Ten Broeke, E., & Renssen, M.R. (1999). Treatment of specific phobias with eye movement desensitization and reprocessing (EMDR): Protocol, empirical Status, and conceptual Issues. *Journal of Anxiety Disorders*, 13(1–2), 69–85.

De Jongh, A. & Ten Broeke, E. (2009). EMDR and the anxiety disorders: Exploring the current status. *Journal of EMDR Practice and Research*, 3(3), 133–140.

Delprato, D.J. (1980). Hereditary determinants of fears and phobias: A critical review. *Behavior Therapy*, 11, 79–103.

Depla, M., ten Have, M., van Balkom, A., & de Graaf, R. (2008). Specific fears and phobias in the general population: results from the

Netherlands mental health survey and incidence study (NEMESIS). *Social Psychiatry & Psychiatric Epidemiology*, 43, 200–208.

Di Nardo, P.A., Guzy, L.T., & Bak, R.M. (1988). Anxiety response patterns and etiological factors in dog-fearful and non-fearful subjects. *Behaviour Research & Therapy*, 26, 245–252.

Dollinger, S.J., O'Donnell, J.P., & Staley, A.A. (1984). Lightening-strike disaster: Effects on children's fears and worries. *Journal of Consulting & Clinical Psychology*, 52(6), 1028–1038.

Eaton, W.W. & Keyl, P.M. (1990). Risk factors for the onset of panic disorder and other panic attacks in a prospective, population-based study. *American Journal of Epidemiology*, 131, 301–311.

Eaton, W.W., Dryman, A., & Weissman, M.M. (1991). Panic and phobia. In L.N. Robins & D.A. Regier (Eds.), *Psychiatric Disorders in America: The Epidemiological Catchment Area Study*. New York: Free Press.

Eisenberger, N.I., Lieberman, M.D., & Williams, K.D. (2003). Does rejection hurt: An fMRI study of social exclusion. *Science*, 302, 290–292.

Emmelkamp, P.M.G. & Wittchen, H.-U. (2009). Specific phobias. In G. Andrews, D.S. Charney, P.J. Sirovatka. & D.A. Regier. (Eds.), *Stress-Induced and Fear Circuitry Disorders Refining the Research Agenda for DSM-V*. Arlington, VA: APA.

Eysenck, H.J. (1979). The conditioning model of neurosis. *Behavioral & Brain Sciences*, 2(2), 155–166.

Faravelli, C., Zucchi, T., viviani, B., Salmoria, R., Perone, A., Paionni, A., Scarpato, A., Vigliaturo, D., Rosi, S., Diadamo, D., Bartolozzi, D., Cecchi, C., & Abardi, L. (2000). Epidemiology of social phobia: A clinical approach. *European Psychiatrist*, 15, 17–24.

Fava, G.A., Rafanelli, C., Grandi, S. et al. (2001). Long-term outcome of panic disorder with agoraphobia treated by exposure. *Psychological Medicine*, 31, 891-898.

Fava, G.A., Rafanelli, C., Tossani, E. & Grandi, S. (2008). Agoraphobia is a disease : a tribute to Sir Martin Roth. *Psychotherapy & Psychosomatics*, 77, 133-138.

Ferguson, T. (1997). Healthcare in cyberspace: Patients lead a revolution. *Futurist*, 31, 29–34.

Field, A.P. (2006). Is conditioning a useful framework for understanding the development and treatment of phobias? *Clinical Psychology Review*, 26, 857–875.

Field, A.P., Argyris, N.G., & Knowles, K.A. (2001). Who's afraid of the big bad wolf? A prospective paradigm to test Rachman's indirect pathways in children. *Behaviour Research & Therapy*, 39, 1259–1276.

Field, A.P. & Lawson, J. (2003). Fear information and the development of fears during childhood: Effects on implicit fear responses and behavioural avoidance. *Behaviour Research & Therapy*, 41, 1277–1293.

Fox, E., Griggs, L., & Mouchlianitis, E. (2007). The detection of fear-relevant stimuli: Are guns noticed as quickly as snakes. *Emotion*, 7(4), 91–696.

Fredrikson, M., Wik, G., Annas, P., Ericson, K., & Stone-Elander, S. (1995). Functional neuroanatomy of visually elicited simple phobic fear: Additional data and theoretical analysis. *Psychophysiology*, 33, 43–48.

Freeman, R. (2005). A dental anxiety scale for children. *British Dental Journal*, 199, 351.

Garcia-Palacios, A., Hoffman, H., See, S., & Botella, C. (2001). Redefining therapeutic success with virtual reality exposure therapy. *Cyberpsychology & Behavior*, 4(3), 341–348.

Geer, J.H. (1965). The development of a scale to measure fear. *Behaviour Research & Therapy*, 3, 45–53.

Gerdes, A.B.M., Uhl, G., & Alpers, G.W. (2009). Spiders are special: Fear and disgust evoked by pictures of arthropods. *Evolution & Human Behavior*, 30, 66–73.

Goodwin, R.D., Faraveli, C., Rosi, S. et al (2005). The epidemiology of panic disorder and agoraphobia in Europe. *European Neuropsychopharmacology*, 15, 435–443.

Graham, J. & Gaffan, E.A. (1997). Fear of water in children and adults: Etiology and familial effects. *Behaviour Research & Therapy*, 35, 91–108.

Grös D.F. & Antony, M.M. (2006). The assessment and treatment of specific phobias: A review. *Current Psychiatry Reports*, 8, 298–303.

Gruppo Italiano Disturbi d'Ansia (1989). Familial analysis of panic disorder and agoraphobia. *Journal of Affective Disorder*, 17, 1–8.

Haidt, J., McCauley, C., & Rozin, P. (1994). Individual differences in sensitivity to disgust: A scale sampling seven domains of disgust elicitors. *Personality & Individual Differences*, 16, 701–713.

Hainsworth, J. & Buchanan, H. (2009). *Clinical Psychology in Dentistry. A Guide to Commissioners of Clinical Psychology Services*. Briefing Paper No. 11. Leicester: The British Psychological Society.

Harris, E.L., Noyes, R., Crowe, R.R. & Chaudry, D.R. (1983). Family study of agoraphobia-report of a pilot study. *Archives of General Psychiatry*, 40, 1061-1064.

Harvey, A. & Rapee, R. (2002). Specific phobia. In D.J. Stein & E. Hollander (Eds.), *Textbook of Anxiety Disorders* (p. 515). Washington, DC: American Psychiatric Publishing, Inc.

Haukebø, K., Skaret, E., Ost, L.G., Raadal, M., Berg, E., Sundberg, H. et al. (2008). One- vs. five-session treatment of dental phobia: A randomized controlled study. *Journal of Behavior Therapy & Experimental Psychiatry*, 39(3), 381–390.

Hayward, C., Wilson, K.A., Lagle, K. et al. (2004). Parent-reported predictors of adolescent panic attacks. *Journal of the American Academy of Child & Adolescent Psychiatry*, 43, 613–620.

Heckelman, L.R. & Schneier, F.R. (1995). Diagnostic issues. In R.G. Heimberg, M.R. Liebowitz, D.A. Hope, & F.R. Schneier (Eds.), *Social Phobia: Diagnosis, Assessment and Treatment* (pp. 3–21). New York: Guilford Press.

Heimberg, R.D., Dodge, C.S., Hope, D.A. et al. (1990). Cognitive behavioural group treatment for social phobia: Comparison with a credible placebo control. *Cognitive Therapy & Research*, 14, 1–23.

Heimberg, R.G., & Barlow, D.H. (1988). Psychosocial treatments for social phobia. *Psychosomatics*, 29, 27–37.

Heimberg, R.G., Salzman, D., Holt, C.S., & Blendell, K. (1993b). Cognitive-behavioral group treatment for social phobia: Effectiveness at 5-year follow-up. *Cognitive Therapy & Research*, 17, 325–339.

Heimberg, R.G. & Juster, H.R. (1995). Cognitive-behavioral treatments: literature review. In R.G. Heimberg, M.R. Liebowitz, D.A. Hope, & F.R. Schneier (Eds.), *Social Phobia: Diagnosis, Assessment and Treatment* (pp. 261–309). New York: Guilford Press.

Hellström, K. & Öst, L.G. (1995). One-session therapist directed exposure vs. two forms of manual directed self-exposure in the treatment of spider phobia. *Behaviour, Research & Therapy*, 33, 959–965.

Hellström, K., Fellenius, J., & Öst, L.G. (1996). One versus five sessions of applied tension in the treatment of blood phobia. *Behaviour Research & Therapy*, 34(2), 101–112.

Herbert, M. (1994). Etiological considerations. In T.H. Ollendick, N.J. King, & W. Yule (Eds.), *International Handbook of Phobic and*

Anxiety Disorders in Children and Adolescents (pp. 3–20). New York: Plenum Press.

Hettema, J.M., Neale, M.C., & Kendler, K.S. (2004). A review and meta-analysis of the genetic epidemiology of anxiety disorders. *American Journal of Psychiatry*, 158, 1568–1578.

Howard, K.E. & Freeman, R. (2007). Reliability and validity of a faces version of the modified child dental anxiety scale. *International Journal of Paediatric Dentistry*, 17, 281–288.

Hudson, J.L. & Rapee, R.M. (2000). The origins of social phobia. *Behavior Modification*, 24, 102–129.

Humphris, G.M., Morrison, T., & Lindsay, S.J.E. (1995). The modified dental anxiety scale: Validation and United Kingdom norms. *Community Dental Health*, 12, 143–150.

Jacobi, F., Wittchen, H.-U, Holting, C., Sommer, S., Lieb, R., Hofler, M., & Pfister, H. (2002). Estimating the prevalence of mental and somatic disorders in the community: Aims and methods of the German national health interview and examination survey. *International Journal of Methods in Psychiatric Research*, 11, 1–18.

Jacobson, N., Follette, W., & Revenstorf, D. (1984). Psychotherapy outcome research: Methods for reporting variability and evaluating clinical significance. *Behavior Therapy*, 15, 336–352.

Janet, P. (1903). *Les obsessions et la psychasthenie*. Paris: Alcan.

Kendler, K.S., Karkowski, L., & Prescott, C. (1999). Fears and phobias: Reliability and heritability. *Psychological Medicine*, 29(3), 539–553.

Kendler, K.S., Gardner, C.O., Annas, P., Neale, M.C., Eaves, L.J., & Lichtenstein, P. (2008). A longitudinal twin study of fears from middle childhood to early adulthood: Evidence for a developmentally dynamic genome. *Archives of General Psychiatry*, 65, 421–429.

Kessler, R.C., Davis, C.G., & Kendler, K.S. (1997). Childhood adversity and adult psychiatric disorder in the US National Comorbidity Survey. *Psychological Medicine*, 27, 1101–1119.

Kessler, R.C., Berglund, P., Demler, O., Jin, R., Merikangas, K.R., & Walters, E.E. (2005). Lifetime prevalence and age-of-onset distributions of DSM-IV disorders in the National Comorbidity Survey Replication. *Archives of General Psychiatry*, 62, 593–602.

Kessler, R.C., Chiu, W.T., Jin, R. et al. (2006). The epidemiology of panic attacks, panic disorder, and agoraphobia in the National Comorbidity Survey Replication. *Archives of General Psychiatry*, 63, 415–424.

Kelin, D.F. (2000). Flawed meta-analyses comparing psychotherapy with pharmacotherapy. *American Journal of Psychiatry*, 157, 1204–1211.

King, K. & Humphris, G.M. (2010). Evidence to confirm the cut-off for screening dental phobia using the Modified Dental Anxiety Scale. *Social Sciences & Dentistry*, 1(1), 21–28.

Klemm,P. & Nolan, M.T. (1998). Internet cancer support groups: Legal and ethical issues for nurse researchers. *Oncology Nursing Forum*, 25, 673–676.

Klieger, D.M. (1987). The snake anxiety questionnaire as a measure of ophidophobia. *Educational & Psychological Measurement*, 47, 449–459.

Kringlen, E., Torgersen, S., & Cramer, V. (2001). A Norwegian psychiatric epidemiological study. *American Journal of Psychiatry*, 158, 1091–1098.

Lang, P.J. (1968). Fear reduction and fear behavior: Problems in treating a construct. In J.M. Schlien (Ed.), *Research in Psychotherapy*, Vol. 3 (pp. 90–103). Washington, DC: American Psychological Association.

Laraia, M.T., Stuart, G.W., Frye, L.H. et al. (1994). Childhood environment of women having panic disorder with agoraphobia. *Journal of Anxiety Disorders*, 8, 1–17.

Lazarus, R.S. & Folkman, S. (1984). *Stress, Appraisal and Coping*. New York: Springer.

LeBeau, R.T., Glenn, D., Liao, B., Wittchen, H.U., Beesdo-Baum, K., Ollendick, T., & Craske, M.G. (2010). Specific phobia: A review of DSM-IV specific phobia and preliminary recommendations for DSM-V. *Depression & Anxiety*, 27, 148–167.

Leibowitz, M.R. (1987). Social phobia. *Modern Problems of Pharmacopsychiatry*, 22, 141–173.

Leibowitz, M.R., Stein, M.B., Tancer, M. et al. (2002). A randomized, double-blind, fixed dose comparison of paroxetine and placebo in the treatment of generalized social anxiety disorder. *Journal of Clinical Psychiatry*, 63, 66–74.

Leung, A.W., Heimberg, R.G., Holt, C.S., & Bruch, M.A. (1994). Social anxiety and perception of early parenting among American, Chinese American and social phobic samples. *Anxiety* 1(2), 80–89.

Lieb, R., Wittchen, H.-U., Hofler, M. et al. (2000). Parental psycho-pathology, parenting styles, and the risk of social phobia in offspring: A prospective-longitudinal community study. *Archives of General Psychiatry*, 57, 859–866.

Liebowitz, M.R., Gorman, J.M., Fyer, A.J., & Klein, D.F. (1985). Social phobia: Review of a neglected anxiety disorder. *Archives of General Psychiatry*, 42, 729–735.

Lincoff, G. & Mitchel, D.H. (1977). *Toxic and Hallucinogenic Mushroom Poisoning*. New York: Van Nostrand, Reinhold.

Lipsitz, J.D. & Schneier, F.R. (2000). Social phobia: Epidemiology and cost of illness. *Pharmacoeconomics*, 18(1), 23–32.

Lobbestael, J., Leurgans, M., & Arntz, A. (2011). Inter-rater reliability of the Structured Clinical Interview for DSM-IV Axis I Disorders (SCID I) and Axis II Disorders (SCID II). *Clinical Psychology & Psychotherapy*, 18, 75–79.

LoBue, V. & DeLoache, J.S. (2008). Detecting the snake in the grass: Attention to fear-relevant stimuli by adults and young children. *Psychological Science*, 19, 284–289.

Locker, D. (2003). Psychosocial consequences of dental fear and anxiety. *Community Dentistry & Oral Epidemiology*, 31, 144–151.

Loftus, E.F. (2004). Memories of things unseen. *Current Directions in Psychological Science*, 13, 145–147.

Madara, E.J. (1997). The mutual-aid self-help online revolution. *Social Policy*, Spring, 20–26.

Magee, W.J., Eaton, W.W., Wittchen, H.-U., McGonagle, K.A., & Kessler, R.C. (1996). Agoraphobia, simple phobia and social phobia in the National Comorbitity Survey. *Archives of General Psychiatry*, 53, 159–168.

Mancini, C., van Ameringen, M., Szatmari, P., Fugere, C. et al. (1996). A high-risk pilot study of the children of adults with social phobia. *Journal of the American Academy of Child & Adolescent Psychiatry*, 35, 1511–1517.

Mannuzza, S., Fyer, A.J., Liebowitz, M.R., & Klein, D.F. (1990). Delineating the boundaries of social phobia: its relationship to panic disorder and agoraphobia. *Journal of Anxiety Disorders*, 4, 41–59.

Marks, I. (1988). Blood-injury phobia: A review. *American Journal of Psychiatry*, 145, 1207–1213.

Marks, I.M. & Gelder, M.G. (1966). Different ages of onset in varieties of phobia. *American Journal of Psychiatry*, 123, 218–221.

Marks, I.M. (1969). *Fears and Phobias*. London: Heinemann.

Marks, I. & O'Sullivan, G. (1988). Drugs and psychological treatments for agoraphobia/panic and obsessive–compulsive disorders: A review. *British Journal of Psychiatry*, 153, 650–658.

Marks, I.M., Kenwright, M., McDonough, M. et al. (2004). Saving clinicians' time by delegating routine aspects of therapy to a computer: A randomized controlled trial in phobia/panic disorder. *Psychological Medicine*, 34, 9–17.

Mathews, A.M., Gelder, M.G., & Johnston, D.W. (1981). *Agoraphobia: Nature & Treatment*. New York: Guilford Press.

Mattick, R.P. & Clarke, J.C. (1998). Development and validation of measures of social phobia scrutiny fear and social interaction anxiety. *Behaviour Research & Therapy*, 36, 455–470.

McLean, C.P. & Hope, D.A. (2010). Subjective anxiety and behavioral avoidance: Gender, gender role, and perceived confirmability of self-report. *Journal of Anxiety Disorders*, 24, 494–502.

McHugh, R.K., Smits, J.A.J., & Otto, M.W. (2009). Empirically supported treatments for panic disorder. *Psychiatric Clinics of North America*, 32, 593–610.

McNally, R.J. (1987). Preparedness and phobias: A review. *Psychological Bulletin*, 101, 283–303.

Meng, C.T.T., Kirkby, K.C., Martin, F., Gilroy, L.J., & Daniels, B.A. (2004). Computer-delivered behavioural avoidance tests for spider phobia. *Behaviour Change*, 21(3), 173–185.

Menzies, R.G. & Clarke, J.C. (1993a). The etiology of fear of heights and its relationship to severity and individual response patterns. *Behaviour Research & Therapy*, 31, 355–365.

Menzies, R.G. & Clarke, J.C. (1993b). The etiology of childhood water phobia. *Behaviour Research & Therapy*, 31, 499–501.

Menzies, R.G. & Clarke, J.C. (1994). Retrospective studies of the origins of phobias: A review. *Anxiety, Stress & Coping*, 7, 305–318.

Menzies, R.G. & Clarke, J.C. (1995). The etiology of acrophobia and its relationship to severity and individual response patterns. *Behaviour Research & Therapy*, 33, 795–803.

Menzies, R.G., Kirkby, K., & Harris, L.M. (1998). The convergent validity of the Phobia Origins Questionnaire: A review of the evidence. *Behaviour Research & Therapy*, 36, 1081–1089.

Merckelbach, H., De Ruiter, C., van den Hout, M.A., & Hoekstra, R. (1989). Conditioning experiences and phobias. *Behaviour Research & Therapy*, 27, 657–662.

Milgrom, P., Vignetisa, H., & Weinstein, P. (1992). Adolescent dental fear and control: Prevalence and theoretical implications. *Behaviour Research & Therapy*, 30, 367–373.

Mineka, S., Davidson, M., Cook, M., & Keir, R. (1984a). Observational conditioning of snake fear in rhesus monkeys. *Journal of Abnormal Psychology*, 93, 355–372.

Mineka, S., Cook, M., & Miller, S. (1984b). Fear conditioned with escapable and inescapable shock: Effects of a feedback stimulus. *Journal of Experimental Psychology: Animal Behavior Processes*, 10, 307–323.

Mineka, S. & Zinbarg, R. (1995). Conditioning and ethological models. In R.G. Heimberg, M.R. Liebowitz, D.A. Hope, & F.R. Schneier (Eds.), *Social Phobia: Diagnosis, Assessment and Treatment* (pp. 134–162). New York: Guilford Press.

Mineka, S. & Zinbarg, R. (1996). Conditioning and ethological models of anxiety disorders: Stress-in-dynamic-context anxiety models. In D. Hope (Ed.), *Perspectives on Anxiety, Panic, and Fear. 43rd Annual Nebraska Symposium on Motivation* (pp. 135–211). Lincoln, NE: University of Nebraska Press.

Mineka, S., Mystkowski, J.L., Hladek, D., & Rodriguez, B.I. (1999). The effects of changing contexts on return of fear following exposure therapy for spider fear. *Journal of Consulting & Clinical Psychology*, 67(4), 599–604.

Mineka, S. & Öhman, A. (2002). Born to fear: Non-associative vs. associative factors in the etiology of phobias. *Behaviour Research & Therapy*, 40, 173–184.

Moore, R., Brødsgaard, I., & Rosenberg, N. (2004). The contribution of embarrassment to phobic dental anxiety: A qualitative research study. *BMC Psychiatry*, 4, 10.

Moynihan, R. (2002). Celebrity selling – part two. *British Medical Journal*, 325, 286.

Mühlberger, A., Wiedemann, G., & Pauli, P. (2003). Efficacy of a one-session virtual reality exposure treatment for fear of flying. *Psychotherapy Research*, 13, 323–336.

Muris, P. & Merckelbach, H. (1996). A comparison of two fear of spider questionnaires. *Journal of Behaviour Therapy & Experimental Psychiatry*, 27(3), 241–244.

Muris, P., Merckelbach, H., de Jong, P.J., & Ollendick, T.H. (2002). The etiology of specific fears and phobias in children: A critique of the non-associative account. *Behaviour Research & Therapy*, 40, 185–195.

Mystkowski, J., Craske, M., & Echiverri, A. (2002). Treatment context and return of fear in spider phobia. *Behavior Therapy*, 33, 399–416.

Neverlien, P.O. (1990). Assessment of a single-item dental anxiety question. *Acta Odontologica Scandinavica*, 48(6), 365–369.

Newton, J.T. & Buck, D.J. (2000). Anxiety and pain measures in dentistry: A guide to their quality and application. *The Journal of the American Dental Association*, 131(10), 1449–1457.

Newton, J.T. & Edwards, J.C. (2005). Psychometric properties of the Modified Dental Anxiety Scale: An independent replication. *Community Dental Health*, 22(1), 40–42.

Öhman, A. (1986). Face the beast and fear the face: Animal and social fears as prototypes for evolutionary analyses of emotion. *Psychophysiology*, 23, 123–145.

Öhman, A. & Mineka, S. (2001). Fears, phobias, and preparedness: Towards an evolved module of fear and fear learning. *Psychological Review*, 108, 483–522.

Ollendick, T.H. & Hirshfeld Becker, D.R. (2002). The development and psychopathology of social anxiety disorder. *Biological Psychiatry*, 51(1), 44–58.

Oosterink, F., de Jongh, A., & Hoogstraten, J. (2009). Prevalence of dental fear and phobia relative to other fear and phobia types. *European Journal of Oral Sciences*, 117, 135–143.

Orr, S.P. & Roth, W.T. (2000). Psychophysiological assessment: Clinical application for PTSD. *Journal of Affective Disorders*, 61, 225–240.

Öst, L-G. & Hugdahl, K. (1981). Acquisition of phobias and anxiety response patterns in clinical patients. *Behaviour Research & Therapy*, 19, 439–447.

Öst, L. -G. & Hugdahl, K. (1985). Acquisition of blood and dental phobia and anxiety response patterns in clinical patients. *Behaviour Research & Therapy*, 23, 27–34.

Öst, L. -G. (1987). Age of onset in different phobias. *Journal of Abnormal Psychology*, 96, 223–229.

Öst, L.G. (1989). One-session treatment for specific phobias. *Behaviour Research & Therapy*, 27, 1–7.

Öst, L.G., Salkovskis, P.M., & Hellström, K. (1991). One-session therapist-directed exposure vs. self-exposure in the treatment of spider phobia. *Behavior Therapy*, 22, 407–422.

Öst, L.G. (1997). Rapid treatment of specific phobias. In G.C.L. Davey (Ed.), *Phobias: A handbook of Theory, Research and Treatment* (pp. 227–247). New York: Wiley.

Öst, L.G., Alm, T., Brandberg, M., & Breitholtz, E. (2001). One vs five sessions of exposure and five sessions of cognitive therapy in the treatment of claustrophobia. *Behaviour Research & Therapy*, 39(2), 167–183.

Peter, H., Bruckner, E., Hand, I., & Rufer, M. (2005). Childhood separation anxiety and separation events in women with agoraphobia with or without panic disorder. *Canadian Journal of Psychiatry*, 50, 941–944.

Pierce, K.A. & Kirkpatrick, D.R. (1992). Do men lie on fear surveys? *Behaviour Research & Therapy*, 30(4), 415–418.

Perugi, G., Simonini, E., Savino, M., Mengali, F., Cassano, G.B., & Akiskal, H.S. (1990). Primary and secondary social phobia: Psychopathologic and familial differentiations. *Comprehensive Psychiatry*, 31, 245–252.

Poulton, R., Thomson, W.M., Davies, S., Kruger, E., Brown, R.H., & Silva, P.A. (1997). Good teeth, bad teeth and fear of the dentist. *Behaviour Research & Therapy*, 35, 327–334.

Poulton, R. & Menzies, R.G. (2002a). Non-associative fear acquisition: A review of the evidence from retrospective and longitudinal research. *Behaviour Research & Therapy*, 40, 127–149.

Poulton, R. & Menzies, R.G. (2002b). Fears born and bred: Toward a more inclusive theory of fear acquisition. *Behaviour Research & Therapy*, 40, 197–208.

Powers, M.B. & Emmelkamp, P.M.G. (2008). Virtual reality exposure therapy for anxiety disorders: A meta-analysis. *Journal of Anxiety Disorders*, 22, 561–569.

Preece, J. (2001). Sociability and usability: Twenty years of chatting online. *Behaviour & Information Technology Journal*, 20, 347–356.

Preece J, Nonnecke B, Andrews D. (2004). The top 5 reasons for lurking: Improving community experiences for everyone. *Computers and Human Behaviour,* 2:201–23.

Purkis, H.M. & Lipp, O.V. (2007). Automatic attention does not equal automatic fear: Preferential attention without implicit valence. *Emotion*, 7, 314–323.

Rachman, S. (1977). The conditioning theory of fear acquisition: A critical examination. *Behaviour Research & Therapy*, 15, 375–387.

Rachman, S. (1990). The determinants and treatment of simple phobias. *Advances in Behaviour Research & Therapy*, 12, 1–30.

Randall, C.L., Thomas, S.E., & Thevos, A.K. (2001a). Concurrent alcoholism and social anxiety disorder: A first step toward developing effective treatments. *Alcoholism: Clinical & Experimental Research*, 25(2), 210–220.

Rapee, R.M. (1995). Descriptive psychopathology of social phobia. In R.G. Heimberg, M.R. Liebowitz, D.A. Hope, & F.R. Schneier (Eds.), *Social Phobia: Diagnosis, Assessment and Treatment* (pp. 41–66). New York: Guilford Press.

Rapee, R.M. & Melville, L.F. (1997). Recall of family factors in social phobia and panic disorder: Comparison of mother and offspring reports. *Depression & Anxiety*, 5, 7–11.

Ray, J., Wide Boman, U., Bodin, L., Berggren, U., Lichtenstien, P., & Broberg, A.G. (2010). Heritability of dental fear. *Journal of Dental Research*, 89, 297.

Regier, D.A., Narrow, W.E., & Rae, D.S. (1993). The de facto US mental and addictive disorders service system: Epidemiologic catchment area prospective 1-year prevalence rates of disorders and service. *Archives of General Psychiatry*, 50(2), 85–94.

Rodriguez, B.I., Craske, M.G., Mineka, S., & Hladek, D. (1999). Context-specificity of relapse: Effects of therapist and environmental context on return of fear. *Behaviour Research & Therapy*, 37(9), 845–862.

Salkovskis, P.M. & Hackmann, A. (1997). Agoraphobia. In G.C.L. Davey (Ed.), *Phobias: A Handbook of Theory, Research & Treatment*. Chichester: Wiley.

Sanderson, A. & Carpenter, R. (1992). Eye movement desensitization versus image confrontation: A single-session crossover study of 58 phobic subjects. *Journal of Behavioural Therapy & Experimental Psychiatry*, 23, 269–275.

Schilder, P. (1938). The social neurosis. *The Psychoanalytic Review*, 25, 1–19.

Schneier, F.R., Johnson, J., Hornig, C.D., Liebowitz, M.R., & Weissman, M.M. (1992). Social phobia: comorbidity and morbidity in an epidemiological sample. *Archives of General Psychiatry*, 49, 282–288.

Schuller, A.A., Willumsen, T., & Holst, D. (2003). Are there differences in oral health and oral health behavior between individuals with high and low dental fear? *Community Dentistry & Oral Epidemiology*, 31, 116–121.

Segrin, C. & Kinney, T. (2005). Social skills deficits among the socially anxious: Rejection from others and loneliness. *Motivation & Emotion*, 19(1), 1–24.

Seligman, M.E.P. (1971). Phobias and preparedness. *Behaviour Therapy*, 3, 307–320.

Skaret, E., Raadal, M., Kvale, G., & Berg, E. (2000). Factors related to missed and cancelled dental appointments among adolescents in Norway. *European Journal of Oral Sciences*, 108, 175–183.

Skinner, B.F. (1974). *About Behaviorism*. New York: Vintage.

Smoller, J.W., Paulus, M.P., Fagerness, J.A., Purcell, S., Yamaki, L.H., Hirshfeld- Becker, D. et al. (2008). Influence of *RGS2* on anxiety-related temperament, personality, and brain function. *Archives of General Psychiatry*, 65, 298–308.

Spencer, R.L. & Hutchison, K.E. (1999). Alcohol, aging and the stress response. *Alcohol Research & Health*, 23(4), 272–283.

Spence, S., Donovan, C., & Brechman-Toussaint, M. (1999). Social skills, social outcomes and cognitive features childhood social phobia. *Journal of Abnormal Psychology*, 108(2), 211–221.

Stangier, U., Heidenreich, T., Peitz, M., Lauterbach, W., & Clark, D.M. (2003). Cognitive therapy for social phobia: Individual versus group treatment. *Behaviour Research & Therapy*, 41, 991–1007.

Stein, M.B. & Kean, Y.M. (2000). Disability and quality of life in social phobia: Epidemiologic findings. *American Journal of Psychiatry*, 157, 1606–1613.

Stemberger, R.T., Turner, S.M., Beidel, D.C., & Calhoun, K.S. (1995). Social phobia: An analysis of possible developmental factors. *Journal of Abnormal Psychology*, 104, 526–531.

Stinson, F., Dawson, D., Chou, S. et al. (2007). The epidemiology of DSM-IV specific phobia in the USA: Result from the National Epidemiologic Survey on alcohol and related conditions. *Psychological Medicine*, 37, 1047–1059.

Tancer, M.E. (1993). Neurobiology of social phobia. *Journal of Clinical Psychiatry*, 54(12), 26–30.

Taylor, J.E., Deane, F.P., & Podd, J.V. (1999). Stability of driving fear acquisition pathways over one year. *Behaviour Research & Therapy*, 37, 927–939.

Tortella-Feliu, M., Botella, C., Llabrés, J., Bretón-López, J.M., del Amo, A.R., Baños, R.M., & Gelabert, J.M. (2011). Virtual reality versus computer-aided exposure treatments for fear of flying. *Behavior Modification*, 35(1), 3–30.

Turner, S.M., Beidel, D.C., Dancu, C., & Stanley, M.A. (1989). An empirically derived inventory to measure social fears and anxiety: the Social Phobia and Anxiety Inventory. *Psychological Assessment*, 1, 35–40.

Wardle, J. (1982). Fear of dentistry. *British Journal of Medical Psychology*, 55(2), 119–126.

Wardle, J., Hayward, P., Higgitt, A., Brewin, C.R., & Gray, J. (1997). Causes of agoraphobia: The patient's perspective. *Behavioural & Cognitive Psychotherapy*, 25, 27–37.

Watson, J. B. & Rayner, R. (1920). Conditioned emotional reactions. *Journal of Experimental Psychology*, 3, 1–14.

Weiller, E., Bisserbe, J.-C, Boyer, P., Lépine, J.P., & Lecrubier, Y. (1996). Social phobia in general health care: An unrecognised undertreated disabling disorder. *British Journal of Psychiatry*, 168, 169–174.

Weissman, M.M. (1993). Family genetics studies of panic disorder. *Journal of Psychiatric Research*, 27, 69–78.

Wells, A. & Clark, D.M. (1997). Social phobia: A cognitive approach. In G.C.L. Davey (Ed.), *Phobias – A Handbook of Theory, Research and Treatment* (pp. 3–26). Chichester: Wiley.

Wheeler, V. (2008). Gillian is terrified of buttons. The Sun, 28 April. Retrieved from: http://www.thesun.co.uk/sol/homepage/news/article1066163.ece.

White, M. & Dorman, S.M. (2001). Receiving social support online: implications for health education. *Health Education Research*, 16, 693–707.

Wik, G., Fredrikson, M., Ericson, K., Eriksson, L., Stone-Elander, S., & Greitz, T. (1993). A functional cerebral response to frightening visual stimulation. *Psychiatry Research: Neuroimaging*, 50, 15–24.

Winzelberg, A.J., Classen, C., Alpers, G.W., Roberts, H., Koopman, C., Adams, R.E., Ernst, H., Dev, P., & Barr Taylor, C. (2002). Evaluation of an internet support group for women with primary breast cancer. *Cancer*, 97, 1164–1173.

Withers, R.D. & Deane, F.P. (1995). Origins of common fears: Effects on severity, anxiety responses and memories of onset. *Behaviour Research & Therapy*, 33, 903–915.

Wittchen, H.-U., Essau, C.A., Zerssen, Dv. et al. (1992). Lifetime and six-month prevalence of mental disorders in the Munich Follow-up Study. *European Archives of Psychiatry & Clinical Neuroscience*, 241, 247–258.

Wittchen, H.-U., Reed, V., & Kessler, R.C. (1998). The relationship of agoraphobia and panic disorder in a community sample of adolescents and young adults. *Archives of General Psychiatry*, 55, 1017–1024.

Wittchen, H.-U., Stein, M.B., & Kessler, R.C. (1999a). Social fears and social phobia in a community sample of adolescents and young adults: prevalence, risk factors and co-morbidity. *Psychological Medicine*, 29, 309–323.

Wittchen, H.-U., Lieb, R., Schuster, P., & Oldehinkel, A.J. (1999b). When is onset? Investigations into early developmental stages of anxiety and depressive disorders. In J.L. Rapoport (Ed.), *Childhood Onset of 'Adult' Psychopathology, Clinical and Research Advances* (pp. 259–302). Washington: American Psychiatric Press.

Wittchen, H.U., Lecrubier, Y., Beesdo, K., & Nocon, A. (2003). Relationships among anxiety disorders: Patterns and implications. In D.J. Nutt & J.C. Ballenger (Eds.), *Anxiety Disorders* (pp. 25–37). Oxford: Blackwell Science.

Wittchen, H.-U., Gloster, A.T., Beesdo-Baum, K., Fava, G.A. & Craske, M.G. (2010). Agoraphobia: A review of the diagnostic classificatory position and criteria. *Depression & Anxiety*, 27, 113-133.

Wolitzky-Taylor, K.B., Horowitz, J.D., Powers, M.B., & Telch, M.J. (2008). Psychological approaches in the treatment of specific phobias: A meta-analysis. *Clinical Psychology Review*, 28, 1021–1037.

Wong, H.M., Humphris, G.M., & Lee, G.T.R. (1998). Preliminary validation and reliability of the Modified Child Dental Anxiety Scale. *Psychological Reports*, 83, 1179–1186.

World Health Organization (1992). *The ICD-10 Classification of Mental and Behavioural Disorders: Clinical Descriptions and Diagnostic Guidelines*. Geneva: World Health Organisation.

Xinyin, C., Rubin, K.H., & Boshu, L. (1995). Social and school adjustment of shy and aggressive children in China. *Development & Psychopathology*, 7, 337–349.

Yartz, A.R. & Hawk, L.W. (2001). Assessment of anxiety: Tales from the heart. In M.M. Antony, S.M. Orsillo, & L. Roemer (Eds.), *Practitioner's Guide to Empirically Based Measures of Anxiety*. Kluwer Academic Press: Plenum Publishers New York.

Zlomke, K. & Davis, T.E. (2008). One-session treatment of specific phobias: A detailed description and review of treatment efficacy. *Behavior Therapy*, 39(3), 207–223.

Index

Reading guide

This table identifies where in the book you'll find relevant information for those of you studying or teaching A-level. You should also, of course, refer to the Index and the Glossary, but navigating a book for a particular set of items can be awkward and we found this table a useful tool when editing the book and so include it here for your convenience.

TOPIC	AQA(A)	AQA(B)	OCR	PAGE
Clinical characteristics	x		x	16
Classification issues	x		x	16
Reliability	x			30
Validity	x			32
Biological explanations	x			57
Genetics	x			57
Biochemistry	x			110
Psychological explanations	x			42, 107, 131
Behavioural	x			35
Cognitive	x			52
Psychodynamic	x			42
Socio-cultural	x			97
Biological therapies	x			67
Agoraphobia		x		121
Social Phobias		x		92